Green Line 2
Das Trainingsbuch

von
Pauline Ashworth

Klett Lerntraining

Zu diesem Trainingsbuch gehört eine Audio-CD. Mit ihrer Hilfe lernst du, Englisch besser zu verstehen. Die Texte sind im Buch mit dem Symbol 🎧 gekennzeichnet. Wenn du die Diktate und Lückendiktate schreibst, benutze die Pausentaste, um Zeit zum Schreiben zu haben. Viel Erfolg!

Sprecher: Samira Aziz, Tariq Aziz, Anna Berry, Gillian Bathmaker, James Heath, Benjamin Martin, Margaret Mills, Colin Mills, Amelie Vollmer, Dominik Vollmer, Marie Louise Vollmer, Amy Walker, Zack Walker
Produktion: Ton in Ton Medienhaus, Stuttgart

Bibliografische Information der Deutschen Nationalbibliothek
Die Deutsche Nationalbibliothek verzeichnet diese Publikation in der Deutschen Nationalbibliografie; detaillierte bibliografische Daten sind im Internet über http://dnb.d-nb.de abrufbar.

Auflage 8 7 | 14 13
Die letzten Zahlen bezeichnen jeweils die Auflage und das Jahr des Druckes.

Das Werk und seine Teile sind urheberrechtlich geschützt. Jede Nutzung in anderen als den gesetzlich zugelassenen Fällen bedarf der vorherigen schriftlichen Einwilligung des Verlages. Hinweis zu §52a UrhG: Weder das Werk noch seine Teile dürfen ohne eine solche Einwilligung eingescannt und in ein Netzwerk eingestellt werden. Dies gilt auch für Intranets von Schulen und sonstigen Bildungseinrichtungen. Fotomechanische Wiedergabe nur mit Genehmigung des Verlages.

© Klett Lerntraining GmbH, Stuttgart 2009. Alle Rechte vorbehalten.
www.klett.de/lernhilfen

Redaktion: form & inhalt verlagsservice Martin H. Bredol/Linda Strehl

Zeichnungen: David Norman, Meerbusch; Lars Benecke, Hannover
Umschlaggestaltung: Koma Amok, Stuttgart
Umschlagfoto: Kerstin Hacker, London
Satz: Meyle+Müller GmbH+Co. KG, Pforzheim
Reproduktion: Meyle+Müller GmbH+Co. KG, Pforzheim
Druck: Mediahaus Biering GmbH, München

Printed in Germany
ISBN 978-3-12-929896-1

Inhalt

Unit 1

In der Schule	6
Verben	7
Die einfache Vergangenheit: unregelmäßige Formen	8
Adjektive	9
Substantive	9
Die einfache Gegenwart: regelmäßige Formen (Wiederholung)	10
Die einfache Vergangenheit: regelmäßige Formen	11
Aussprache und Schreibung der einfachen Vergangenheit	12
Die Aussprache von *-ed*	12
Die einfache Vergangenheit von *to be*	13
Die einfache Vergangenheit: unregelmäßige Formen	15
Zuhören und Schreiben	15
Die Verneinung der einfachen Vergangenheit mit *didn't*	16
Fragen mit *did* und Kurzantworten	18
Fragen mit Fragewörtern und *did*	20
Informationen heraussuchen	21
Das Wesentliche verstehen	22
Hören und wiederholen	23
Hören und das Wesentliche verstehen	23
Hören und Informationen heraussuchen	24
Hören und zuordnen	24

Unit 2

In London	25
U-Bahn fahren	26
Unregelmäßige Verben: Infinitiv und Vergangenheit	27
Anagramme	28
Eine Stadt beschreiben	28
Die Verlaufsform und die einfache Form der Gegenwart (Wiederholung)	29
Die Verlaufsform der Vergangenheit	30
Zuhören und schreiben	32
Die Steigerung von Adjektiven mit *-er* und *-est*	33
Die Steigerung von Adjektiven mit *more* und *most*	34
Der Vergleich im Satz	35
Das Stützwort *one/ones* nach Adjektiven	37
Have und *have got*	38
Zuhören: *have* und *have got*	39
Informationen heraussuchen	40
Das Wesentliche verstehen	41
Hören und schreiben	42
Hören und verstehen	42
Hören und Informationen heraussuchen	43
Hören und zuordnen	43

Unit 3

Einkaufen	44
Verben, die mit Geld zu tun haben	45
Unregelmäßige Verben	45
Adjektive	46
Some und *any*	46
Essen: Auswärts oder daheim?	47
Fragen mit *do/did* (Wiederholung)	48
Bestätigungsfragen	49
Die Zusammensetzungen von *some* und *any*	51
Some in Fragen	52

Every und seine Zusammensetzungen	53
No und seine Zusammensetzungen	54
Das *Going-to*-Futur	55
Lesen und verstehen	57
Das Wesentliche verstehen	58
Zuhören: Bestätigungsfragen	59
Zuhören und schreiben	59
Zuhören und ordnen	60
Zuhören und verstehen	60

Revision A (Unit 1–3)

Schule und Mahlzeiten	61
Essen	62
Einkaufen gehen	62
Verben: Gegenteile und Vergangenheitsformen	63
Vergangenheit, Gegenwart und Zukunft	64
Kommunikationsübung	65
Hörverstehen	66
Schreiben	66

Unit 4

Musik und Stars	67
Wichtige Wendungen	67
Rechtschreibung	68
Verben	69
Das unregelmäßige Partizip Perfekt	70
Signalwörter	70
Die einfache Vergangenheit (Wiederholung)	71
Das Perfekt: regelmäßige und unregelmäßige Formen	72
Das Partizip Perfekt	73
Das Perfekt: Fragen und Kurzantworten	74
Signalwörter für das Perfekt	76
Das Perfekt und die einfache Form der Vergangenheit	77
Zuhören und verstehen	77
Das Wesentliche verstehen	79
Einzelheiten verstehen	80

Zuhören und zuordnen	81
Zuhören	81
Zuhören und verstehen	82

Unit 5

Sport	83
Was man beim Sport braucht	84
Gesundheit	84
Menschen	85
Der Körper	85
Adjektive: Menschen beschreiben	86
Verben: fit bleiben	86
Die Fragewörter *who*, *what* und *which*	87
Fragen mit Fragewörtern und Präpositionen	89
Adverbien der Art und Weise	90
Adjektiv oder Adverb?	91
Die Steigerung des Adverbs	92
Lesen und einen Bericht schreiben	93
Informationen heraussuchen	94
Hören und verstehen	95
Hören und zuordnen	96
Hören und Informationen heraussuchen	96

Revision B (Unit 4–5)

Jobs	97
Körperteile, Krankheit und Sport	97
Verben	98
Das Perfekt und die einfache Vergangenheit	99
Übersetzung	100
Schreiben und Zuhören	101

Unit 6

In Schottland	102
Das Wetter	103
Freiheitskampf	103
Menschen beschreiben	104
Verben	104
Gefühle ausdrücken	105

Wichtige Ausdrücke: rund ums Postamt	105	Einfache Vergangenheit und Perfekt	130
Die Possessivpronomen	106	*May*, *could* und *shall*	130
Possessivbegleiter oder Possessivpronomen?	106	Die Verlaufsform der Vergangenheit	131
Das *Will*-Futur	107	Bedingungssätze in der einfachen Gegenwart	132
Die Verneinung des *Will*-Futurs; Fragen mit Kurzantwort	108	Das *Will*-Futur und das *Going-to*-Futur	132
Zuhören	109	Fragen	132
Gegenüberstellung: das *Will*-Futur und das *Going-to*-Futur	110	Besser formulieren	133
Bedingungssätze in der einfachen Gegenwart	112	Übersetzung: Beim Arzt	134
Gegenüberstellung: *if* und *when*	114	Zuhören und Verstehen	134
Lesen und Charaktere beschreiben	115	Eine Postkarte schreiben	135
Zuhören	117	Zuhören: Wichtige Wendungen	135
Zuhören und Informationen heraussuchen	117		
Zuhören und schreiben	118	**Lösungen**	136
Zuhören und das Wesentliche verstehen	118		

Unit 7

Mit dem Flugzeug unterwegs	119
Reise nach England	120
Welt und Weltraum	121
Verben	121
Die modalen Hilfsverben *may*, *could* und *shall*	122
Lesefähigkeit: Broschüren lesen	124
Lesen und das Wesentliche verstehen	125
Zuhören und Einzelheiten verstehen	126
Zuhören	126
Zuhören und das Wesentliche verstehen	127

Revision C (Unit 6–7)

Reisen	128
Adjektive: Menschen und Handlungen beschreiben	128
Verben: Sprechen	129
Adjektiv oder Adverb?	129

1 | Wortschatz | Grammatik | Leseverstehen | Hörverstehen

Unit 1

In der Schule

1 Lies dir die Wörter durch, dann übersetze sie.

register _____   planner _____

assembly _____   timetable _____

break _____   library _____

2 In dem Wortgitter verstecken sich neun Schulfächer. Schreibe sie heraus und übersetze sie.

M	A	T	H	S	P	H	B	N
F	R	E	N	C	H	I	M	B
D	E	C	C	I	U	S	O	I
I	S	H	P	E	Q	T	K	O
T	H	N	X	N	E	O	A	L
Z	M	O	W	C	D	R	Q	O
N	L	L	R	E	F	Y	W	G
G	E	O	G	R	A	P	H	Y
O	X	G	E	F	H	E	T	I
P	Q	Y	L	B	C	R	E	U

_____

_____

_____

_____

Wortschatz 1

Verben

3 Vervollständige das Kreuzworträtsel mit den fehlenden Verben.

1. I'd like a green door. Can I … it?
2. Those sandwiches look good. Can I … one?
3. I often … at my aunt's house in the summer.
4. What time do you usually … at school?
5. I don't want to … a school uniform.
6. I don't copy her homework but we … our answers.

4 Übersetze diese Verben. Achtung: Manchmal brauchst du mehrere Wörter.

verlieren _____

sich rächen _____ _____ _____

die Anwesenheit kontrollieren _____ _____ _____

überprüfen _____

(Schulfach) belegen _____

ausradieren _____ _____

bezahlen _____

in Schwierigkeiten geraten _____ _____ _____

Tipp Schreibe die englische Wendung auf die eine Seite einer Karteikarte, die deutsche Bedeutung auf die andere Seite und teste dich selbst!

1 Wortschatz | Grammatik | Leseverstehen | Hörverstehen

Die einfache Vergangenheit: unregelmäßige Formen

5 Suche die neun Verben aus der Wortschlange heraus und ergänze dazu die Form der einfachen Vergangenheit.

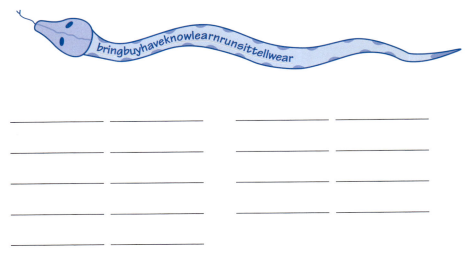

_____ _____   _____ _____

_____ _____   _____ _____

_____ _____   _____ _____

_____ _____   _____ _____

_____ _____

6 Im Schulunterricht. Welche Verben in der Vergangenheit fehlen in diesen Sätzen?

I d _ _ my homework yesterday.

I f _ _ _ _ _ my school books. They were under my bed.

I s _ _ a dog at school today. It was in the playground.

My mum c _ _ _ _ to school today. She wanted to talk to my tutor.

I w _ _ _ _ a story in French today.

I w _ _ _ to assembly this morning.

I w _ _ late for school today.

I g _ _ a new planner yesterday.

Adjektive

7 Baue aus den Wortteilen sechs Adjektive zusammen und schreibe sie in die richtige Lücke.

embar	po	wond	str	ha	nega
or	rd	rassing	erful	tive	ict

I was late for assembly and then I fell over a chair. It was so _____.

My holiday wasn't just good. It was _____.

Don't be so _____. I think it's really good.

I don't like our R.E. teacher. He's too _____.

Our homework isn't easy. It's really _____.

His parents aren't rich. They're _____.

Substantive

8 Ein Ferienbericht. Welche Substantive gehören in die Lücken?

I had a great summer. First I painted my room with some green p _ _ _ _. It looks interesting. Then we went to Wales on holiday and I tried a _ _ _ _ _ _ _ _. That was great and a little scary. Then I went swimming in the sea and saw a s _ _ _ _. That wasn't so great and it was very scary. We stayed on a c _ _ _ _ _ _ _. That was fun and we were lucky because the weather was good all week. A baker lived near the campsite and one day I helped him make some b _ _ _ _. The evenings were boring sometimes but one evening we saw a p _ _ _ that was really funny.

Die einfache Gegenwart: regelmäßige Formen (Wiederholung)

Erinnere dich: *He, she, it* – das *s* muss mit!
I **like** chocolate. She **walks** to school. They **live** in London.
Fragen bildest du mit *do* oder *does* vor dem Subjekt:
Do you play tennis? – **Yes, I do.**
What **does he do?** – He **plays** football.
Mit *don't* oder *doesn't* verneinst du Sätze:
I **don't watch** TV in the evening.
He **doesn't eat** chocolate.

9 Am Wochenende. Ergänze die Verben in der richtigen Form.

Gordon: What _____ (you/do) on Saturday mornings?

Kevin: I _____ (help) my mum in the house or I _____

(meet) some friends.

Gordon: _____ (your sister/help) your mum, too?

Kevin: No, _____ *(Kurzantwort)*. She _____

(work) in my dad's shop.

Gordon: _____ (she/like) it?

Kevin: Yes, _____ *(Kurzantwort)*. Well, my dad

_____ (give) her some money and she likes that. I _____

_____ (not work) in the shop because my dad says

I'm too young.

Gordon: Oh, and what _____ (you/do) on Sundays?

Kevin: We often _____ (go) to the park and my sister often

_____ (go) shopping and buys things with the money

from my dad.

Grammatik 1

Die einfache Vergangenheit: regelmäßige Formen

Wenn du über etwas sprechen willst, was in der Vergangenheit passiert ist und abgeschlossen ist, verwendest du das *simple past*:
Yesterday I **walked** to school.
You **called** me at home last night.
She **watched** a good film at the weekend.
They **jumped** in the sea on holiday.

10 Ferien zuhause. Trage die richtige Vergangenheitsform der Verben an der passenden Stelle ein.

listen   paint   play   stay   visit   watch

We _stayed_ at home in the summer but the holidays weren't boring. We _painted_ our rooms blue, _played_ football in the park and _visited_ our friends. We often went to London and we _watched_ to some good bands in Covent Garden and we _listened_ a play in a park. Yes, our holidays were great.

11 Am Wochenende. Übersetze diese Sätze.

1. Am Samstag blieb ich zuhause.

_____

2. Am Nachmittag besuchten mich meine Freunde.

_____

3. Wir redeten und lachten im Garten bis um 17 Uhr.

_____

_____

Aussprache und Schreibung der einfachen Vergangenheit

Beim Sprechen:
Nach **stimmhaften** Konsonanten spricht man [d]: played, climbed
Nach **stimmlosen** Konsonanten spricht man [t]: talked, finished
Nach [d] oder [t] spricht man [ɪd]: needed, visited

Beim Schreiben:
Das stumme End-*e* fällt weg: to believe ⟶ **believed**
Verben auf Konsonant + *y* enden mit *-ied:* to carry ⟶ **carried**
Endkonsonanten nach kurzen Vokalen werden gedoppelt: to stop ⟶ **stopped**

12 Am Strand. Ergänze die richtigen Vergangenheitsformen.

We (arrive) _____ at the beach at ten. We (park) _____ the car and we (carry) _____ our bags to the beach. We (play) _____ football and our dog (chase) _____ some birds. He (try) _____ to catch one but they were too fast. When we (stop) _____ for lunch, we saw that the sea was now very near. "It's coming in," (say) _____ my brother. We (finish) _____ our lunch on the wall.

Die Aussprache von *-ed* 🔊 1

13 Schreibe die Vergangenheitsformen der angegebenen Verben in die richtige Spalte. Höre dir dann auf der CD an, ob du sie richtig zugeordnet hast.

climb – need – paint – talk – smile – start – stop – try – watch

[d]	[t]	[ɪd]
_____	_____	_____
_____	_____	_____
_____	_____	_____

Die einfache Vergangenheit von *to be*

Im *simple past* gibt es zwei Formen von *to be*:
I/he/she/it **was** eleven last year.
You/we/they **were** happy yesterday.
Were you at home last night? – Yes, I **was.**
Was it cold at the weekend? – No, it **wasn't.** It **was** really warm.
Were your friends with you? – No, they **weren't.** They **weren't** in town yesterday.

14 Wer hat das Fahrrad gestohlen? Bilde Fragen und Antworten aus den angegebenen Wörtern.

were – lunchtime – where – you – yesterday – ?

_____

library – I – was – the – in

_____

lunchtime – you – were – the – bike sheds – at – in – ?

_____

school – we – at – weren't – yesterday

_____

Chris – in – at – the – 12 o'clock – bike sheds – was

_____

your – wasn't – in – bike – bike shed – the

_____

it – in – your – was – garden

_____

15 Was war gestern um 8 Uhr los? Formuliere Fragen und Kurzantworten.

_____ in the kitchen? – Yes,
_____ .

Mary – kitchen

_____ ? – No,
_____ .

Paul – ~~in bed~~

_____ ? –
_____ .

Henry and Liz – happy

_____
_____ ? – _____ .

Bill and David – ~~classroom~~

16 Morgenversammlung. Übersetze die folgende Unterhaltung.

Warst du heute Morgen in der Versammlung? – Ja.

_____

_____

War sie gut? – Naja, sie war nicht interessant, aber sie war kurz.

_____

_____

Die einfache Vergangenheit: unregelmäßige Formen

Die regelmäßigen Verben im *simple past* enden alle auf *-ed*. Die unregelmäßigen Verben haben verschiedene Formen, die du einfach auswendig lernen musst. Hier sind einige der wichtigsten:

to have → I **had** a good holiday in France this summer.
to go → You **went** to school on Monday.
to get → He **got** a bike for his birthday.
to find → We **found** a bag two days ago.
to see → I **saw** a good film last night.

17 In den Ferien. Setze die Verben in die richtige Vergangenheitsform. Achtung: Eines musst du zweimal verwenden.

come – do – find – get – go – have – tell

I _____ a great holiday in the summer. We _____ to France and we stayed there on a campsite for two weeks. The weather was good and we _____ lots of nice things there. One day I _____ some money. I _____ my sister and she wanted to keep it. I was very good and _____ the woman at the campsite. The next day a man _____ to me and said thank you. He was very nice so I was happy, but the best thing was – I _____ ten euros, too.

Zuhören und Schreiben

18 Höre dir die Sätze an und schreibe sie auf. Kreuze die Sätze an, die in der Vergangenheit sind.

_____ ☐
_____ ☐
_____ ☐

Die Verneinung der einfachen Vergangenheit mit *didn't*

Die einfache Gegenwart verneinst du mit *don't* oder *doesn't* + Infinitiv. Bei der einfachen Vergangenheit verwendest du einfach ***didn't* + die Grundform des Verbs:**
I **didn't have** a good holiday.
Liz **didn't buy** me a present.
We **didn't go** to school yesterday.
They **didn't eat** the cake.

19 Bilde aus den angegebenen Wörtern Aussagesätze.

didn't – I – my – ride – bike

_____

play – we – football – at – didn't – lunchtime

_____

morning – in – John – didn't – the – go – swimming

_____

laugh – my – at – you – jokes – didn't

_____

meet – my – I – the – friends – didn't – afternoon – in

_____

we – we – got – go – late – and – up – didn't – to – school

_____

Was hast du gestern gemacht, was hast du nicht gemacht? Schreibe zur Übung ein paar Sätze auf.

20 Sieh dir die Bilder an, dann formuliere, was gestern passiert oder nicht passiert ist.

They _____

I _____

The dog _____

We _____ games.

21 Brian hat in den Ferien das Gegenteil von dem gemacht, was Sarah getan hat. Was hat er gemacht und was nicht?

1. Sarah went to France.

   _____

2. Sarah didn't have good weather.

   _____

3. Sarah stayed at a campsite.

   _____

4. Sarah didn't find a dog.

   _____

5. Sarah had a good time.

   _____

Fragen mit *did* und Kurzantworten

Frage	Kurzantwort
Did you **like** your present?	Yes, I **did**./No, I **didn't**.
Did Alan **eat** the last cake?	Yes, he **did**./No, he **didn't**.
Did it **rain** yesterday?	Yes, it **did**./No, it **didn't**.
Did your friends **find** you?	Yes, they **did**./No, they **didn't**.

22 John hat den ersten Schultag verpasst. Am folgenden Tag fragt er seine Freunde, wie es war. Ergänze die Kurzantworten.

Did you all get a new timetable?   Yes, _____

Did Christine arrive late?   No, _____

Did the teachers give you lots of homework?   No, _____

Did you like your new tutor, Liz?   Yes, _____

23 Williams Mutter stellt ihm Fragen zum ersten Schultag. Bilde aus den Wörtern Fragen in den richtigen Wortstellung.

get – did – a – new – you – planner – ?

_____

new – teachers – books – give – did – you – your – ?

_____

assembly – you – did – listen – in – ?

_____

eat – did – all – your – your – friends – sandwiches – ?

_____

Grammatik 1

24 Bevor Lisas Mutter zur Arbeit geht, gibt sie Lisa eine Liste mit Dingen, die sie erledigen soll. Als sie wiederkommt, fragt sie Lisa, was sie davon gemacht hat. Schreibe einen Dialog mit Fragen und Kurzantworten.

wash the car ✓

phone Aunt Jean ✗

walk the dog ✓

make a birthday card ✗

Mum: _____

Lisa: _____

Mum: _____

Lisa: _____

Mum: _____

Lisa: _____

Mum: _____

Lisa: _____

25 Paul und Tina unterhalten sich über die Ferien. Trage das Verb in der richtigen Form in die Lücken ein.

Paul: _____ (you/go) on holiday?

Tina: No, _____. I _____ (stay) at home.

Paul: Oh, but _____ (you/have) a good time?

Tina: Yes, _____, but the weather was terrible.

It _____ (rain) a lot. _____ (you/go) away?

Paul: Yes, _____. We _____ (go) to Australia.

Tina: Oh great. _____ (you/like) it?

Paul: Yes, _____, but the weather was terrible there, too.

Tina: Really? But it _____ (not/rain) in Australia!

Paul: Yes, _____. It was winter there.

Fragen mit Fragewörtern und *did*

Fragewort	did	Subjekt	Infinitiv	restlicher Satz
Where	did	you	go	yesterday?
What	did	Chris	buy	at the shops?
When	did	we	arrive	at the party?
Who	did	the boys	meet	in town?

26 Zoe ist aus den Ferien zurück. Formuliere zu ihren Antworten die Fragen, die Owen ihr stellt. Tipp: Die Fragen beziehen sich auf den unterstrichenen Satzteil.

Owen: _____ on holiday?

Zoe: We went <u>to France</u>.

Owen: _____ with?

Zoe: I went with <u>my parents, my brothers and a friend</u>.

Owen: _____ to France?

Zoe: We went <u>by car</u>.

Owen: _____ there?

Zoe: We <u>went swimming and played on the beach</u>.

Owen: _____

Zoe: We arrived home <u>last night</u>.

Owen: _____ best?

Zoe: I liked <u>the food</u>.

Informationen heraussuchen

27 Adrian muss einen Aufsatz über seinen ersten Schultag schreiben. Lies seinen Text, dann beantworte die Fragen mit *right* oder *wrong*.

My first day at my new school
Last year we lived in Germany and I went to school in my town there. It was nice. I liked school and all my friends lived there, too, of course. Now we live in England and yesterday was my first day at my new school here. I was scared before I went to school because I didn't know the pupils there, but I liked it.
The best thing was that school started at quarter to nine and so I got up at quarter to eight. That was nice. I knew that all my friends in Germany were at school and I was still in bed!
Of course, I was still at school at three o'clock when all my German friends were at home, but that wasn't too bad. There are lots of interesting clubs after school and I want to go to bastketball club and to computer club next week.
In the morning they often have assembly but they didn't have it yesterday. We had a lesson with our tutor and she gave us our timetable and new planners. Our first lesson was German. That was funny. All the pupils said German is so hard but I can't understand that at all. Then we had a drama lesson and we all acted a funny thing that happened in the summer holidays.
At half past twelve we all had lunch in the cafeteria. I went with Jenny and Tim, my new friends, and lunch was … OK! In the afternoon we had Science and Art. I liked the lessons and the teachers are OK, too, but there's one thing that I don't like at all. Yes, you guessed it – it's the school uniform.

1. Adrian lives in Germany. _____

2. School started at 8.45. _____

3. School finished after three o'clock. _____

4. Adrian went to basketball club. _____

5. They had assembly yesterday. _____

6. He liked the drama lesson. _____

7. He had lunch at school. _____

8. He likes the school uniform. _____

| 1 | Wortschatz | Grammatik | **Leseverstehen** | Hörverstehen |

Das Wesentliche verstehen

28 Sommerferien! Lies zuerst die Unterhaltung, dann stelle die Textabschnitte in die richtige Reihenfolge.

A
Yvonne: Well, my parents wanted to go in museums and churches all day.
Mark: But museums can be interesting.
Yvonne: Yes, I know. One or two museums in a summer is OK but I think I saw twenty museums.
Mark: Oh no. Well, did you have a good time in Wales?
Yvonne: Yes, that was great. I went on an adventure holiday there.
Mark: An adventure holiday? What's that?

B
Yvonne: Yes, we did. And what did you do in the summer?
Mark: Oh, I went on an adventure holiday, too.
Yvonne: Did you? Where did you go?
Mark: I went to Poland and that was a real adventure.
Yvonne: Why?
Mark: We don't speak Polish.

C
Mark: Hi Yvonne. Did you have a good summer?
Yvonne: Yes, it was good. I went to Italy with my parents and then I went to Wales.
Mark: Oh, Italy. That's nice.
Yvonne: Well, it wasn't so good. The food was good and the weather was good but the holiday was a bit boring.
Mark: Boring? Why?

D
Yvonne: Oh, we did lots of sports. We tried abseiling and we sailed and climbed.
Mark: Wow. I'd like to try that. Was it good?
Yvonne: Yeah. It was great.
Mark: Did your parents go, too?
Yvonne: No, it was just for people from 11 to 14. All the girls slept in one bedroom and all the boys in another. And we had parties at night with candles and cakes.
Mark: Did you stay for a week?

Richtige Reihenfolge der Textabschnitte: _____

Hörverstehen 1

Hören und wiederholen 3

29 Höre dir die Fragen auf der CD an und lies mit, dann sprich sie nach.

+ Did you have a nice holiday?

– Yes, I did. I had a great time.

+ Where did you go?

– We went to France.

+ What did you do there?

– We visited some friends and we went swimming in the sea.

Hören und das Wesentliche verstehen 4

30 Chris ist zu spät dran. Höre dir das Gespräch zwischen ihr und ihrer Mutter an, dann schau dir den Stundenplan an. Welcher Tag ist heute?

Period	Monday	Tuesday	Wednesday	Thursday	Friday
1	Maths	Science	Music	English	Science
2	R.E.	Maths	Technology	P.E.	English
			Break		
3	Technology	English	Science	Maths	Geography
4	French	Geography	History	German	French
			Lunch		
5	Art	P.E.	Drama	History	History

Today is _____.

Hören und Informationen heraussuchen

31 Nach den langen Sommerferien trifft Ellen Tim in der Schule wieder. Höre zu und entscheide, ob diese Sätze *wrong* oder *right* sind.

1. The weather was bad all summer. _____
2. Ellen's friends stayed at home all summer. _____
3. Ellen didn't enjoy the summer holidays. _____
4. Tim enjoyed the summer holidays. _____
5. Tim went on holiday in the summer. _____
6. Tim worked in his summer holidays. _____
7. Tim painted walls, worked in gardens and went shopping. _____
8. Tim worked because he needed the money. _____

Hören und zuordnen

32 Neil und Fiona sprechen über die vergangenen Sommerferien. Höre dir erst den Dialog an, dann ordne jeweils das Verb des Satzes der richtigen Aussprache zu.

[d]	[t]	[ɪd]
_____	_____	_____
_____	_____	_____
_____	_____	_____

Holidays, here I come!

24

Unit 2

In London

1 Was gibt es in London zu tun oder sehen? Welche Wörter fehlen in den Sätzen?

The Tate Modern is a famous g _ _ _ _ _ _. They have a lot of pictures there.

Buckingham P _ _ _ _ _ is the home of the Royal Family.

The London D _ _ _ _ _ _ is a museum of horror.

You can see a play at one of London's many t _ _ _ _ _ _ _ _.

When you want to get somewhere, use the T _ _ _.

Most tourists go s _ _ _ _ _ _ _ _ _ _.

Did you know you can also go i _ _ s _ _ _ _ _ _ _ in London?

2 Suche die sieben gefragten Wörter aus dem Wortgitter und ordne sie richtig zu.

Three things you can find in a street:

_____

Two things you can find in a museum:

_____

Two things you can find in a palace:

_____

q	p	u	k	o	i	b	t
d	i	n	o	s	a	u	r
d	g	z	s	k	j	s	a
k	e	w	q	e	s	k	f
o	o	g	u	i	d	e	f
p	n	y	e	s	g	r	i
c	a	s	e	a	f	m	c
j	k	i	n	g	b	e	n

U-Bahn fahren

3 Ian und Ken möchten zum London Eye. Wie kommen sie dorthin? Vervollständige den Dialog.

Ian: Let's _ _ _ _ the Central Line.

Ken: OK. And where _ _ _ _ we _ _ _ _ _ _ trains?

Ian: At Tottenham Court Road. And we must _ _ _ _ _ a southbound train. Then it's three _ _ _ _ _ to Embankment.

Ken: Must we _ _ _ _ _ _ at Embankment?

Ian: Yes, we can walk from there.

4 Trage die gesuchten Wörter in die Kästchen ein. Die Buchstaben in den grauen Feldern ergeben das Lösungswort.

1. A person who travels on the tube is a …
2. Trains have many …
3. A … is a special ticket.
4. You wait on a … when you want to take a train.
5. The … is how much you pay for a ticket.
6. When you travel on the Tube, you must have a …
7. Let's get off at the next …

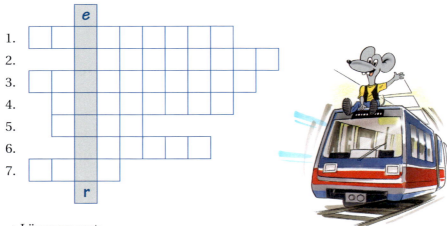

→ Lösungswort: _____

Unregelmäßige Verben: Infinitiv und Vergangenheit

5 Vervollständige die Tabelle.

infinitive	simple past	German infinitive
to begin	_____	_____
_____	caught	_____
_____	_____	hinfallen
to find out	_____	_____
_____	flew	_____
_____	_____	verletzen
to leave	_____	_____
_____	spent	_____

6 Schlecht gelaufen? Wähle jeweils ein Verb im *simple past* aus Aufgabe 5 und ergänze die Lücken. Achtung: Eines steht nicht in der Tabelle!

My day _____ at seven and then everything went wrong. I was sitting on a wall and waiting for a new friend in Trafalgar Square when a pigeon _____ too near me and I _____. I _____ my hand and _____ my clothes all dirty, so I went to the nearest shop and bought some more. I _____ an hour in the shop and when I went back to Trafalgar Square, I was late, and my new friend was there. He was talking and laughing with another girl. When the next bus _____ Trafalgar Square, I was on it. Well, my new clothes are nice and the boy wasn't – so maybe it wasn't a bad day.

2 | Wortschatz | Grammatik | Leseverstehen | Hörverstehen

Anagramme

7 Anagramme sind Wörter, bei denen die Buchstaben durcheinandergeraten sind. Schreibe das richtige Wort neben die Definition.

tanique   repefum   begetlave   tfiru   hwtac   prape

You can write on this. _____

This is very old. _____

You can eat this and it's often sweet. _____

You should eat one or two of these every day. _____

You can wear this and it has a good smell – usually. _____

Look at this when you want to know the time. _____

Eine Stadt beschreiben

8 Finde sieben Adjektive und ergänze damit die Sätze.

best exciting full high popular rainy true

London is a very _____ city. Lots of people like it and many tourists go there every year. It's also very _____ because there are lots of different people there and you can do so many different things. For example, you can go on the London Eye. It's very _____ and you get a great view of London.

People think that England is always _____ but they are wrong. It doesn't rain often in London. It's _____ that there are millions of people in London and the buses and trains are often _____, but I like that. I think London is the _____ city in England.

Grammatik 2

Die Verlaufsform und die einfache Form der Gegenwart (Wiederholung)

Das **simple present** verwendest du bei gewohnheitsmäßigen Handlungen:	Das **present progressive** verwendest du, wenn eine Handlung gerade abläuft:
I **like** chocolate. She always **gets up** at 7 o'clock. und bei aufeinanderfolgenden Handlungen: They **play** football and then **eat** their lunch in the cafeteria. Signalwörter sind *always, often, never, sometimes*.	I'**m sitting** on a bus now. Look! That man **is painting** a picture on the wall. What **is** that woman **doing** over there? We **aren't meeting** today. Signalwörter sind *Look!, now, at the moment, today*.

9 Ein Tag in der Stadt. Schreibe die richtige Form des Verbs in die Lücken.

John ___goes___ (go) to London every year. He loves it. He always ___goes___ (go) shopping because he knows some great music shops there, and he always ___listens___ (listen) to the buskers in Covent Garden. This year John is in London again but this time everything is different. It ___begins___ (begin) the same. He ___takes___ (take) the train to London with his friends and then they go to Covent Garden. They go and watch the buskers when suddenly he ___sees___ (see) a girl he knows from school. The girl is ___playing___ (play) a guitar now and she ___is singing___ (sing). It's beautiful and lots of people ___listen___ (listen). When she ___finishes___ (finish), John talks to her. They go and ___have___ (have) a drink in a café together. They ___are walking___ (walk) together in Hyde Park now but he ___doesn't see___ (not/see) the people there.

Die Verlaufsform der Vergangenheit

Du verwendest das *past progressive*, um zu sagen, was an einem bestimmten Punkt in der Vergangenheit gerade passierte und noch nicht abgeschlossen war:
What **were you doing** at seven o'clock?
I **was helping** my mum.
Ellen and Liz **were doing** their homework.
We **weren't watching** TV.
Man verwendet es oft zusammen mit dem *simple past*.

past progressive – gerade ablaufende Handlung:	*simple past* – neues Ereignis:
I **was eating** my dinner, *Ich habe gerade gegessen,*	when **Paul called**. *als Paul anrief.*
While we **were watching** a play, *Während wir ein Theaterstück angeschaut haben,*	a **mobile phone rang**. *klingelte ein Handy.*

10 Mitternacht. Ergänze die richtige Form des Verbs.

What ___were you doing___ (you/do) at 12 o'clock last night?

I ___was reading___ (read) a scary book.

My brothers ___were looking for___ (look for) monsters under the bed.

My dad ___was working___ (work).

My older sister ___was dancing___ (dance) in a disco.

We ___weren't sleeping___ (not/sleep) but we didn't hear the thieves.

They ___were driving___ (drive) our car away.

11 Ein Brand in London. Bilde ganze Sätze, indem du die Wörter in die richtige Reihenfolge bringst.

while – started – was – sleeping – the fire – the baker's family

_____

they – the house – the next house – when – the fire – were – jumped – leaving – to

_____

were – they – lost – getting – their houses – neighbours – while – water

_____

burning – two days – was – of London – later – a large part

_____

12 Ein Besuch im Buckingham Palace. Verbinde die Satzteile.

I was walking though London	while I was sitting in a living room.
While I was taking a photo,	I was sitting at my desk at home.
She was walking in the garden	William was swimming in it.
She showed me her house	while we were waiting for the tea.
When I saw the swimming pool,	the Queen arrived.
I fell asleep	when she invited me for a cup of tea.
When I woke up,	when I saw Buckingham Palace.

Wenn der Satz mit *while* oder *when* anfängt, kommt ein Komma nach dem ersten Satzteil. Steht der *while*- oder *when*-Satzteil als Zweites, wird kein Komma verwendet.

Zuhören und schreiben 7

13 Im Hyde Park. Welche Handlung läuft gerade ab, was ist ein neues Ereignis? Bilde jeweils zwei Sätze: einen mit *when* und einen mit *while*.

1. he – break his leg – they – play football

   <u>While they   </u>

   _____

2. the woman – ride a horse – her mobile – ring

   _____

   _____

3. the man – listen to his radio – he – fall asleep

   _____

   _____

14 London ist manchmal klein. Ergänze die richtigen Formen der Verben.

I _____ (travel) to Covent Garden on the Tube when I _____ (meet) a friend. While we _____ (talk), the train _____ (stop) at Covent Garden. The doors _____ (close) when my friend _____ (say), "Didn't you want to get off here?" I got off and the train _____ (leave) when I _____ (remember) that my bag was still on the train. My mobile phone, my money and my travel card were in the bag. I was just thinking, "What can I do now?" when I _____ (see) another friend. One phone call and ten minutes later I had my bag again.

Grammatik 2

Die Steigerung von Adjektiven mit *-er* und *-est*

	Grundform	Komparativ	Superlativ
alle einsilbigen Adjektive:	old nice	older nicer	the oldest the nicest
zweisilbige Adjektive auf *-y*:	silly happy	sillier happier	the silliest the happiest
einige zweisilbige Adjektive:	quiet simple	quieter simpler	the quietest the simplest

- Ein Endkonsonant wird nach einem kurzen Vokal verdoppelt: big – bigger – the biggest
- Ein stummes *-e* am Ende entfällt: late – later – the latest
- Wenn ein Adjektiv auf Konsonant + *-y* endet, wird das *-y* zu *-i*: lucky – luckier – the luckiest
- Nach *-ng* wird zusätzlich ein [g] gesprochen: long [lɒŋ] – longer ['lɒŋɡə] – the longest ['lɒŋɡɪst]

Good und *bad* sind unregelmäßig: **good – better** – the **best**; **bad – worse** – the **worst**

15 Vervollständige die Tabelle.

Grundform	Komparativ	Superlativ
little	littler	littlest
sweet	sweeter	sweetest
scary	scarier	the scariest
safe	safer	safest
lucky	more lucky	most lucky
big	bigger	the biggest
good	better	the best

Die Steigerung von Adjektiven mit *more* und *most*

Mit *more* und *most* werden gesteigert:
- die meisten zweisilbigen Adjektive, die nicht auf -y enden,
- alle drei- oder mehrsilbigen Adjektive:

Grundform	Komparativ	Superlativ
boring	**more** boring	**the most** boring
interesting	**more** interesting	**the most** interesting

16 Lies den Text und schreibe die zehn Adjektive heraus. Dann vervollständige die Tabelle mit dem entsprechenden Komparativ und Superlativ.

Mat is very lucky. He lives in a big house in an exciting and beautiful city. He's got a new bike and lots of money. He likes school and his teachers are good. Mat's popular, but today he isn't happy. He's nervous. He's got a Maths test and Mat is bad at Maths.

Grundform	Komparativ	Superlativ

Der Vergleich im Satz

Wenn zwei Dinge **gleich** sind, formulierst du so:

The cat is as fast as the dog.	Die Katze ist so schnell wie der Hund.
Ann is as excited as Tom.	Ann ist so gespannt wie Tom.

Wenn zwei Dinge **ungleich** sind, drückst du es so aus:

The cat is faster than the mouse.	Die Katze ist schneller als die Maus.
Liz is more excited than Ann.	Liz ist gespannter als Ann.
The mouse is not as fast as the cat.	Die Maus ist nicht so schnell wie die Katze.
Ann is not as excited as Liz.	Ann ist nicht so gespannt wie Liz.

17 Schau dir die Bilder an und vervollständige die Sätze.

1. big

   The horse _____ the pig.

   The pig _____ the horse.

2. excited

   The boy _____ the girl.

3. 30 p / 20 p / £ 1.20 — expensive

   The chocolate _____ the apple.

   The chocolate _____ the sandwiches.

   The sandwiches _____ expensive.

4. bought in 2006 / bought in 2006 — new

   The computer _____ the bike.

2 | Wortschatz | Grammatik | Leseverstehen | Hörverstehen

18 Ein Besuch in London. Trage die passenden Wörter ein.

Glenda: I love London. It's so much more exciting _____ our town.

Paul: Yes, but it's _____ expensive, too.

Glenda: Oh no. There are lots of shops that aren't as _____ in our town. You can buy some really cheap clothes in London.

Paul: True. And the museums are really _____, too.

Glenda: Yes, they are _____ interesting museums in England, I think.

Paul: But do you know _____ best thing in London?

Glenda: Er. Covent Garden? The buskers there are really good.

Paul: Yes, they are _____ the buskers at home. But the best thing is that my favourite football team plays here.

19 Graham hat zwei Schwestern, Janet und Tina. Formuliere weitere Vergleiche.

1. Graham is older than Janet and Janet is older than Tina.

    Graham _____ Tina.

    Tina _____ Janet.

    Graham _____.

2. Tina is more popular than Graham and Janet is more popular than Tina.

    Graham _____ Tina.

    Janet _____ Graham.

    Janet _____.

Das Stützwort *one/ones* nach Adjektiven

Wenn du ein Nomen nicht wiederholen möchtest, brauchst du statt dessen **one/ones,** denn im Englischen kann ein Adjektiv nicht alleine stehen.
Which is your house? – The biggest **one.**
Those shoes are nice. – Yes, and the red **ones** are the nicest.

20 Auf dem Markt. Ergänze *one* oder *ones*.

How much are the apples? – The green _____ or the red _____?

Which T-shirt do you want? – The green _____.

Which bag do want to look at? – The big brown _____.

How much are those sandwiches? – These cheese _____ are £1.50.

21 Im Souvenirladen. Übersetze die unterstrichenen Teile der Kurzdialoge.

1. Was kosten die Postkarten? – <u>Die großen kosten 30 Pence.</u>

_____

2. Mir gefällt das Sweatshirt. – <u>Möchtest du dieses weiße anprobieren?</u>

_____

3. Kann ich bitte das T-Shirt anprobieren? – <u>Dieses gelbe?</u>

_____

4. Das Poster ist lustig. – <u>Das kleine an der Wand?</u>

_____

5. Die Schuhe sind schön. – <u>Meinst du die blauen?</u>

_____

Have und *have got*

Das Verb *have* kann wie das Verb *have got* „haben" oder „besitzen" bedeuten.
Rob has got a computer.   Rob has a computer.
Have you got a computer?   Do you have a computer?

Da es keine Vergangenheit des Verbs *have got* gibt, muss man *had* verwenden:
Rob had a computer.   Did you have a computer?

Es gibt auch bestimmte **feste Ausdrücke** mit *have*. Hier kann man *have got* nicht verwenden:
He's **having** a bath.   Er badet.
Did you **have fun** yesterday?   Hast du gestern Spaß gehabt?
I always **have breakfast** at 8.   Ich frühstücke immer um 8.
Have a good time.   Viel Spaß!

22 Gib die folgenden Sätze mit dem Verb *have* wieder.

Have you got a map of London?

Do you have a map of London?

She's got a nice new T-shirt.

Does she have a nice new T-shirt.

I haven't got any money.

I don't have any money.

London has got lots of cheap shops and markets.

_____

23 Formuliere diese Sätze mit dem Verb *have got* um. Achtung: Nicht überall ist das möglich!

1. I had a nice day yesterday.

   _____

2. London has many stations.

   _____

3. They're having a picnic.

   _____

4. I don't have a ticket.

   _____

5. I had a bath this morning.

   _____

Zuhören: *have* und *have got* 8

24 Höre dir die Sätze an und ordne sie der richtigen Überschrift zu.

have:

_____

_____

_____

have got:

_____

_____

_____

Informationen heraussuchen

25 Wenn du einen Text hast, der viele Informationen enthält, liest du ihn am besten mehrfach. Folge den Anweisungen der Reihe nach.

A. Lies den Text einmal schnell durch und finde eine Überschrift dafür.
B. Lies die Fragen zum Text, dann lies den Text noch einmal sorgfältig durch.
C. Beantworte die Fragen.

Überschrift: _____

Camden Lock Market
Camden Lock Market is open every day but there are more stalls open at the weekend. You can buy almost everything here from food to furniture and clothes of course, cheap or designer. It's great for a day out because you can sit in one of the cafés by the canal and watch boats go by. It opens at 10 am and closes at 6 pm.

Madame Tussauds Wax Museum
Here you can meet all the people who you want to meet. Let your friends take your photo with the Queen, kiss Brad Pitt or say hello to William Shakespeare. You can also find out about London's history or sing with Justin Timberlake. It's open every day.

Hyde Park
When you want to relax, come to Hyde Park. It's London's biggest park. You can have a picnic on the grass, sit in a café or just watch the people here. Some people even ride horses here.

1. Can you buy tables at Camden Lock Market? _____
2. Where can you see famous people? _____
3. Is Hyde Park bigger than Regent's Park? _____
4. Where can you watch boats? _____
5. Are there cafés in Hyde Park? _____
6. Where can you see horses? _____
7. Where can you find out about the history of London? _____
8. Can you go to Camden Lock Market on Sundays? _____

Leseverstehen 2

Das Wesentliche verstehen

26 Ein Tagesausflug nach London. Welche Überschrift passt am besten zu welchem Absatz?

Two buskers! _____   Where can we go? _____

A day at Covent Garden _____   Help! I'm not a tourist. _____

A.
It was summer and Lisa's cousin, Patrick, was staying with them for a week.
"Let's go on the London Eye today," said Lisa.
"But aren't there always big queues in the holidays?" asked Patrick.
"Oh yes, of course. Well. How about the Tower of London?"
"Oh no, I haven't got any money. Let's go to Covent Garden again," said Patrick.

B.
They went to Covent Garden again. It was their favourite place. They liked the markets and they loved the buskers and they liked laughing at the tourists. First they walked round the market and looked at the clothes. Then they bought a drink and some chips and sat down outside and listened to a busker.
"I'd love to be a busker," said Patrick.
"Oh no. I love singing but I don't want to sing in front of all those people."
"But why? You're really good at singing."

C.
The buskers finished and some street theatre started. They were really funny and Patrick and Lisa were near the front. Suddenly an actor wanted Lisa to help with a trick. She threw balls to him while he was sitting on a big unicyle *(Einrad)*. Of course, the man didn't catch the balls and he fell off his unicycle.
All the people laughed. It was all a trick, of course, but when Lisa went back to Patrick, she just said, "Oh, it was so embarrassing. That usually just happens to tourists." While she was talking to Patrick, a thief took her bag.

D.
They were walking back to a Tube station when Lisa said, "Oh no, where's my bag?" They went back and looked for it but they couldn't find it.
"What can we do now? Do you want to tell the police?" said Patrick.
"No. It was almost empty. But my travelcard was in it and a little money. Can you buy me a ticket, Patrick?"
"Oh, Lisa, I'm really sorry, I haven't got any money now."
They thought for a while and then Patrick said, "I know. We can be buskers."
"Oh, Patrick you can't do this to me."
"Come on. We can sing a few songs and then we can buy a ticket."

2 | Wortschatz | Grammatik | Leseverstehen | Hörverstehen

Hören und schreiben 9

27 „Entschuldigung, wo …?" Höre zu und ergänze die fehlenden Wörter.

+ Excuse me, can you _____ to the nearest Tube station?

− Yes, go _____ on and then _____ the first left into Penny Lane.

+ Excuse me, _____ can _____ St Paul's?

− _____ the Northern Line to Bank and _____ Central Line. You _____ a westbound train and _____.

Hören und verstehen 10

28 Höre dir die CD an und finde heraus, wo diese Leute hinwollen.

1. _____ 3. _____

2. _____ 4. _____

Hörverstehen 2

Hören und Informationen heraussuchen 🎧 11

29 Anders als geplant. Höre zu, dann beantworte die Fragen mit *right* oder *wrong*.

1. Wendy wanted to watch a film in the afternoon. _____
2. She fell while she was running to the bus stop. _____
3. Wendy hurt her arm when she fell. _____
4. The doors closed before Wendy got to the ticket machine. _____
5. She was walking in Leicester Square when a man asked her a question. _____
6. The tourist wanted to walk to Covent Garden. _____
7. Wendy went with the tourist to Covent Garden. _____
8. They both watched a busker. _____

Hören und zuordnen 🎧 12

30 Heute ist Samstag. Über welche Sehenswürdigkeiten wird gesprochen?

Madame Tussauds Adult: £ 14.00 to £ 25.00 per ticket Child: £ 9.00 to £ 21.00 per ticket Open all year Mon – Fri 9.30 am – 5.30 pm; Sat, Sun 9.00 am – 6.00 pm	**Art Gallery** Adult: £ 10.00 Child: £ 5.00 Open all year Mon – Fri 9.00 am – 5.00 pm; Sat, Sun 9.00 am – 6.00 pm
British Museum *1 January 2007 to 31 December 2007* *Every Mon – Wed, Sat, Sun 10.00 am – 5.30 pm;* *Thu, Fri 10.00 am – 8.30 pm* *Adult: £ 0.00 per ticket*	**London Eye** 1 Jun – 30 Sep 2007 Daily 10.00 am – 9.00 pm Adult: £14.50 to £29.50 per ticket Child: £7.25 to £9.00 per ticket

1. _____   2. _____   3. _____

Unit 3

Einkaufen

1 Vervollständige das Rätsel.

1. What does that skirt …, please?
2. Excuse me, where's the …?
3. Thank you and here's your …
4. How much do you … every week?
5. I love going …
6. I don't like the … of those trousers.
7. My money's in my …
8. The shop … is looking for my size.
9. I looked at the … before I tried it on.
10. I've got no … on my mobile.

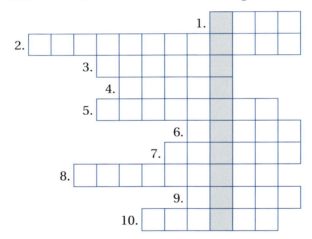

You can pay with this when you have got no money: _____

2 Beschrifte die Gegenstände.

1. _____
2. _____
3. _____
4. _____
5. _____
6. _____

Verben, die mit Geld zu tun haben

3 Bilde aus den Wortteilen Verben, setze sie in die einfache Vergangenheit und trage sie in den richtigen Satz ein.

sa	ea	bor	le	spe	co
nd	ve	st	rn	row	nd

On Saturday I worked in my dad's shop and _____ five pounds.

I _____ Sue five pounds last week but she still hasn't got any money.

Last year I always _____ too much but this year I'm much better.

I _____ some money every week last year and now I've got £ 200.

These trainers were expensive. They _____ £ 35.

I _____ some money from dad yesterday because I wanted to buy mum a present.

Unregelmäßige Verben

4 Übersetze die Verben und ergänze ihre einfache Vergangenheitsform.

stehlen	_to_ _____	_____
werden	_____	_____
denken	_____	_____
lesen	_____	_____
schütteln	_____	_____

Adjektive

5 Sortiere die Buchstaben zu Adjektiven, die menschliche Eigenschaften beschreiben.

1. eamn: He's _____. He never spends his money.

2. orlberih: She's _____. She's never nice to me.

3. grevissage: He's _____. He often hits people.

4. yreged: She's _____. She always eats too much.

5. lopupra: He's _____. Everybody likes him.

Some und *any*

6 Beim Essen. Übersetze die Sätze.

Hat jemand Hunger?

_____

Möchtest du etwas essen?

_____

Kann mir bitte jemand helfen?

_____

Alles ist fertig. Kommt zu Tisch.

_____

Ich kann meine Gabel nirgends finden.

_____

Auf dem Tisch befindet sich nichts. (!)

_____

Wortschatz 3

Essen: Auswärts oder daheim?

7 Beschrifte die Gegenstände auf den Bildern.

1. _____
2. _____
3. _____
4. _____
5. _____
6. _____
7. _____
8. _____
9. _____
10. _____
11. _____
12. _____
13. _____

8 Was muss man vor, was nach dem Essen tun? Vervollständige die Wendungen.

to l _ _ t _ _ t _ _ _ _   to c _ _ _ _ t _ _ t _ _ _ _   to w _ _ _ u _

Fragen mit *do/did* (Wiederholung)

Fragen mit Vollverben *(to play, to eat, to walk, to think)* im *simple present* werden mit *do* oder *does* gebildet:
Do you play tennis? – Yes, I do.
What **does she like?** – She likes chocolate.
Fragen mit Vollverben im *simple past* werden mit *did* gebildet:
What **did you do** yesterday? – I went to town.
Did John eat my cake? – Yes, he did. He ate it all.

9 Bilde zu den Antworten die entsprechenden Fragen.

– It was your birthday yesterday, wasn't it?

  What _____ (do)?

+ We went to that French restaurant.

– _____ (like) it?

+ Yes, it was great. I love French food.

– _____ (go) there often?

+ Yes, we do. We often go when it's somebody's birthday.

– Who _____ (go) with this year?

+ I went with my family and my cousin, Robert, came, too.

– Oh, he lives in France, doesn't he? _____ (visit) you

  every year on your birthday?

+ No, he doesn't. But his dad's working here this week so

  he came with him.

– _____ (like) it here?

+ Yes, he does, but he doesn't like the food.

Bestätigungsfragen

Du verwendest *question tags*, wenn du erwartest, dass man dir zustimmt. *Question tags* entsprechen im Deutschen den Ausdrücken „nicht wahr?", „oder?".

bejahter Aussagesatz [+]	question tag [−]	verneinter Aussagesatz [−]	question tag [+]
Ann is popular,	isn't she?	Ann isn't nice,	is she?
Rob can ride,	can't he?	Rob can't drive,	can he?
We've got P.E.,	haven't we?	We haven't got R.E.,	have we?
You like chocolate,	don't you?	You don't like meat,	do you?
Dad often works,	doesn't he?	Dad doesn't like it,	does he?
You had a picnic,	didn't you?	You didn't eat here,	did you?

Du bildest Bestätigungsfragen mit dem Subjekt und dem Hilfsverb des vorangehenden Satzes. Wenn es kein Hilfsverb gibt, verwendest du das Hilfsverb, mit dem du eine Frage bilden würdest. Wenn der Aussagesatz bejaht ist, verneinst du die Bestätigungsfrage. Wenn er verneint ist, bejahst du sie.

10 Beim Shoppen. Verbinde die Aussagesätze mit den richtigen *question tags*.

You have got some money,   aren't they?

They're nice,   can we?

That isn't expensive,   didn't you?

You bought some new trainers yesterday,   doesn't he?

You don't like that skirt,   do you?

Your dad often gives you money,   haven't you?

We can't have credit cards,   isn't it?

That's really beautiful,   is it?

11 Fragen rund ums Geld. Trage die richtigen *question tags* ein.

You can't save money, _____?

Rebecca earns some money every week, _____?

I'm not mean, _____?

You haven't got any money, _____?

You borrowed some money from me last week, _____?

You often borrow money, _____?

Tom's parents bought him a new bike, _____?

Tom's lucky, _____?

12 Im Café. Ergänze die passenden *question tags* und die Antworten dazu.

Luca: That looks good, _____?

Sophie: Yes, _____. But you don't like meat, _____?

Luca: No, _____. But it isn't meat, _____?

Sophie: Yes, I think, it is. That waiter doesn't want to bring us the menu, _____?

Luca: No, _____. But we aren't doing anything wrong, _____?

Sophie: No, _____. And we can eat here, _____?

Luca: Yes, if we want to. But we don't want to eat here, _____?

Sophie: No, we don't. Let's go.

Die Zusammensetzungen von *some* und *any*

Zusammensetzungen mit **some** verwendest du in bejahten Sätzen:
Somebody/someone is at the door.
My book is **somewhere** in my room.
I need **something** to wear.

Zusammensetzungen mit **any** verwendest du in verneinten Sätzen und Fragen:
Has **anybody/anyone** got some money?
I haven't got **anything** in my bag.
I can't find my book **anywhere.**

13 Ergänze die richtigen Zusammensetzungen mit *some* oder *any*.

In the kitchen

Dad: It's lunchtime and I'd like _____ to lay the table, please.

Pete: Oh, I'm hungry. Is there _____ tasty for lunch?

Dad: I always make _____ tasty for lunch.

In the living room

Kylie: I want to buy Ginny _____ for her birthday but I can't

think of _____. Has _____ got an idea?

Mum: Look in your magazine. Maybe you can find _____ in

there.

Kylie: Has _____ got my magazine? I can't find

it _____.

Mum: It must be _____. You were reading it yesterday.

Pete: Here's your magazine, but there isn't _____

interesting in it.

Some in Fragen

> Normalerweise verwendest du *any* in Fragen, aber wenn du eine positive Antwort erwartest, kannst du auch *some* oder eine Zusammensetzung mit *some* verwenden. Es handelt sich dann eigentlich um eine Bitte, ein Angebot oder einen Vorschlag:
> Can somebody help me, please?
> Can I have something to eat, please? → Bitte
> Would you like some crisps? → Angebot
> Can we go somewhere to eat? → Vorschlag

14 Bitte, Angebot, Vorschlag oder Frage? Lies zunächst die Sätze und trage deine Entscheidung rechts ein. Vervollständige dann die Sätze auf der linken Seite mit *some*, *any* oder einer Zusammensetzung.

Would you like _____ to eat? _____

Let's go _____ nice on Saturday. _____

Has _____ got my book? _____

Can you lend me _____ money, please? _____

Can I have _____ water, please? _____

Can _____ help me, please? _____

Can _____ see my bag? _____

Can I help you with _____? _____

In Sätzen, die mit *Would you like …?* oder *Can I have …?* beginnen, verwendet man normalerweise *some*.

Every und seine Zusammensetzungen

Ähnlich wie bei *some* und *any* gibt es auch Zusammensetzungen mit *every*:

I know **everybody** in my class.   Ich kenne alle in meiner Klasse.
John runs **everywhere**.   John läuft überall.
We ate **everything** on the table.   Wir aßen alles auf, was auf dem Tisch war.

15 Übersetze diese Sätze.

Jeder leiht ihr Geld.

_____

Er findet überall Geld.

_____

Ich will immer alles kaufen.

_____

16 Schreibe *every*, *some*, *any* oder eine Zusammensetzung in die Lücken.

1. *Graham:* Can I borrow _____ money, Dad?

   Dad: Why? You don't need _____ money, do you?

   We buy you _____.

2. *Dad:* _____ always wants to borrow money from me.

   Michelle: I don't want to borrow _____ money, Dad.

   I want you to give me _____.

No und seine Zusammensetzungen

No kannst du vor Nomen verwenden:
I've got **no** money.   Ich habe kein Geld.

Auch mit *no* kann man Zusammensetzungen bauen:
Nobody loves me.   Niemand liebt mich.
Nowhere is nicer than here.   Nirgendwo ist es schöner als hier.
My dog's ill. He ate **nothing** for lunch.   Mein Hund ist krank. Mittags fraß er nichts.

17 Wochenende! Trage *no, nothing, nobody* oder *nowhere* ein.

Chris: What did you do at the weekend?

Neil: _____. It was really boring. There was _____ here and I had _____ to do.

Chris: Oh, and there was _____ on television, was there?

Neil: No, and we have _____ videos.

Chris: So what did you do? You can't do _____.

Neil: No, I did my homework!

18 Ein Geschenk aussuchen. Ergänze *some, any, no, every* oder eine Zusammensetzung.

It's difficult to find a present when you've got _____ money

and you haven't got _____ ideas. I went to town yesterday

and I looked _____ for a present for Angela and I couldn't

find _____. I asked _____ for their ideas

but _____ had _____. Then I had an idea.

What is it? I'm not telling _____. It's a surprise.

54

Grammatik 3

Das *Going-to*-Futur

Du verwendest das *Going-to*-Futur, wenn du sagen willst, was du vorhast, also Pläne hast, oder wenn du schon absehen kannst, was passieren wird. Wenn du z. B. aufstehst und der Himmel wolkenlos ist, sagst du: It's going to be warm today.

What **are** you **going to do** today? – We**'re going to meet** some friends.	Was hast du heute vor? – Wir wollen/werden ein paar Freunde treffen.
What **is** Ann **going to do**? – She**'s going to mend** her bike.	Was hat Ann vor? – Sie wird ihr Fahrrad reparieren.

Kurzantworten werden mit einer Form von *be* gebildet:
Are we **going to eat** now? – Yes, **we are.**
Is Tom **going to call**? – No, **he isn't.**

19 Samstagnachmittag. Was haben diese Leute vor oder nicht vor?

1. She _____ the bill.

pay

2. She _____ a burger.

eat

3. They _____ a game.

play

4. They _____ dinner.

eat

5. He _____ his room.

clean

55

20 Gemma hat Geburtstag. Trage die richtigen Formen des *Going-to*-Futur ein.

Paul: What _____ (you/do) on your birthday, Gemma?

Gemma: I _____ (have) a party at home. Would you like to come?

Paul: Yes, please. _____ (you/have) it in the garden?

Gemma: Yes, _____ *(Kurzantwort)*, if it doesn't rain.

Paul: And _____ (sister/come)?

Gemma: No, _____ *(Kurzantwort)*. She _____ _____ (meet) her friends. And my parents _____ _____ (not/be) there. They don't know it yet, but they _____ (stay) in their room upstairs.

21 Übersetze diesen kleinen Dialog.

Ellen: Hast du vor, zum Mittagessen Spaghetti zu kochen?
Mum: Nein. Ich koche heute nichts.
Ellen: Was werden wir dann essen?
Mum: Ihr könnt Sandwiches essen. Ich esse in einem Restaurant.
Ellen: Oh, Mama! Das ist nicht fair!

Ellen: _____ for lunch?

Mum: _____. _____ anything today.

Ellen: What _____?

Mum: You can have sandwiches. I _____ in a restaurant.

Ellen: Oh, Mum. That's not fair.

Lesen und verstehen

22 Was macht Steve am Wochenende? Lies den Text und beantworte die Fragen.

Emily: What are you going to do at the weekend?
Steve: I'm going to visit my grandma.
Emily: Oh, she lives in Manchester, doesn't she?
Steve: Yes, she does.
Emily: So what are you going to do there?
Steve: We're going to go shopping. There are some great shops in Manchester.
Emily: But how are you going to buy anything? You never have any money.
Steve: Yes, I know, but my grandma's going to give me some.
Emily: Is she? That's nice of her.
Steve: Yes, well, it was my birthday last week.
Emily: Oh yes, it was on Thursday, wasn't it?
Steve: Yes, it was, and so she's going to give me my present at the weekend.
Emily: And what are you going to buy?
Steve: Oh, I don't know. Maybe a Discman or new trainers and I'd like a new mobile.
Emily: Er, Steve, and maybe you can give me my money back, too.
Steve: Your money?
Emily: Yes, I lent you 20 pounds last week. You remember, don't you?
Steve: Oh no. I forgot about that.

1. What's Steve going to do at the weekend? _____

   _____

2. Has Steve got any money? _____

3. Why is his grandma going to give him some money? _____

   _____

4. What does Steve want to buy? _____

   _____

5. What must he do with his money? And why? _____

   _____

Das Wesentliche verstehen

23 Was hat Sarah letzte Woche gemacht? Lies die Kurzdialoge und ordne ihnen die passende Situation zu.

Sarah ordered a drink in a café.
The waiter brought Sarah the wrong food.
Sarah tries some trousers on.
Sarah can't find her size.

A: _____
Sarah: Excuse me. Where are the changing rooms, please?
Woman: They're over there. Would you like to try those on?
Sarah: Yes, please.
Woman: Were they OK?
Sarah: Yes, they're great. How much are they, please?
Woman: Er. They're £45.99.

B: _____
Sarah: Excuse me.
Man: Yes, can I help you?
Sarah: Yes, I'm sorry, but this is the wrong salad. I ordered the salad with cheese.
Man: Oh, I'm very sorry. Just wait a minute, please.

C: _____
Woman: Hello. Can I help you?
Sarah: Yes, please. I'm looking for some green trousers.
Woman: There are some over here.
Sarah: They're nice.
Woman: What size do you need?
Sarah: Size 12.
Woman: Oh, I'm sorry. We've only got size 10 or size 14.

D: _____
Sarah: Can you bring us the menu, please?
Woman: Yes, of course. Here it is.
Sarah: Can you tell me what this is, please?
Woman: Yes, it's a fish. Can I get you anything to drink while you are looking at the menu?
Sarah: Oh, yes. I'd like a glass of water, please.

Zuhören: Bestätigungsfragen 🎧 13

24 Beim Shoppen. Höre dir die Bestätigungsfragen an und zeichne mit einem Pfeil ein, ob die Stimme dabei nach oben oder nach unten geht.

Those trousers are nice, aren't they?

You aren't going to buy those, are you?

You can't take all those in the changing rooms, can you?

Jean doesn't wear trainers, does she?

Tipp: Erinnere dich: Wenn deine Stimme nach oben geht, bedeutet es, dass du nicht sicher bist. Wenn deine Stimme nach unten geht, stellst du lediglich eine Bestätigungsfrage.

Zuhören und schreiben 🎧 14

25 Im Café. Sieh dir den Dialog an und überlege, welches Wort oder welche Wörter in die Lücken passen. Dann höre dir die CD an und trage die richtigen Wörter ein.

Tom: _____. Can you _____ the menu,

_____? And _____ a glass of water and

a cup of tea, please.

Waitress: Yes, of course. (…) Here are your drinks and here's the menu.

Tom: _____. The glass of water is _____. And

can you _____ what _____ is?

Waitress: Yes, it's chicken and chips.

Tom: OK. Then _____ the special and my grandma

_____ the salad, _____.

Zuhören und ordnen 🎵 15

26 Schau dir zunächst die Wörter an, dann höre sie dir an und spreche sie nach. In welche Spalte gehören sie? Höre nochmals zu und überprüfe deine Antworten.

back – bread – hang – have – lend – said – salad – spend

[e]	[æ]
_____	_____
_____	_____
_____	_____
_____	_____

Zuhören und verstehen 16

27 Höre dir die zwei Dialoge an und beantworte danach die Fragen.

Dialogue A:

1. Where is the girl? _____

2. What does she want to try on? _____

3. Does she want to buy them? _____

4. Is she polite? _____

Dialogue B:

1. Where is the girl? _____

2. What is today's special? _____

3. What does she want to eat? _____

4. Is she polite? _____

Revision A (Unit 1–3)

Schule und Mahlzeiten

1 Sieh dir zunächst die Wörter an, dann vervollständige die Mindmap.

assembly – break – fork – fruit – History – knife – meat – P. E. – plate – Science – spoon – subject – tutorial – vegetables

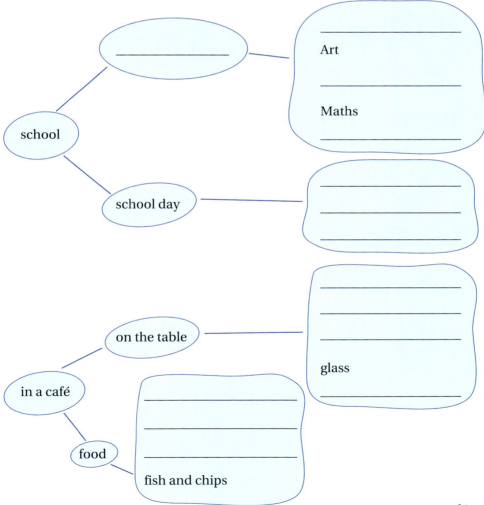

Essen

2 Beschrifte die Abbildungen.

1.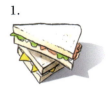
2.
3.
4.

_____ _____ _____ _____

5.
6.
7.
8.

_____ _____ _____ _____

Einkaufen gehen

3 Finde den Begriff, der jeweils nicht in die Gruppe passt.

1.
to buy
to pay
to spend
to save

→ _____

2.
trousers
skirt
trainers
change

→ _____

3.
waitress
shop assistant
changing room
waiter

→ _____

4.
antique
supermarket
perfume
skirt

→ _____

Verben: Gegenteile und Vergangenheitsformen

4 Löse die Anagramme auf und ordne sie ihrem Gegenteil zu.

to lose ⟷ _____

to sell ⟷ _____

to arrive ⟷ _____

to get off ⟷ _____

to cry ⟷ _____

to borrow ⟷ _____

to save ⟷ _____

to come ⟷ _____

og
hgaul
teg no
pensd
ndfi
deln
veale
yub

5 Ergänze den Text mit den Vergangenheitsformen der Verben aus Aufgabe 4.

What a day! I got up late and _____ the house. I ran to the station and _____ the train – the wrong train. I changed trains and I _____ to town. I wanted to meet my friend Jane in a café at 12.30, but first I needed a birthday present. I went to my favourite shop and _____ her a really nice present. Then I bought a few presents for me, too. I _____ all my money and then walked to the café. In the café Jane _____ me some money for a drink and then I wanted to give Jane her birthday present but where was my bag? I didn't have it. Jane looked at me and _____. Then she said, "Are you looking for this? I _____ it in your favourite shop."

Vergangenheit, Gegenwart und Zukunft

6 Geburtstag. Schreibe die richtige Zeitform des angegebenen Verbs in die Lücken.

"What _____ (you/do) next Saturday?" I asked my friends at school. "I _____ (mend) my bike," said Ann. "And you _____ (visit) your grandma, aren't you, Mike?" I wanted to meet them because it was my birthday on Saturday but I _____ _____ (not/tell) them. It _____ (be) my first year at school and so they didn't know it was my birthday. I _____ (wake up) early on Saturday morning and I _____ (get) some nice birthday presents from my mum and dad and my brother but I was sad. I wanted to meet my friends.

I _____ (watch) TV at about 4 o'clock when my mum said, "Can you walk the dog, please, Chris?" It _____ (rain) and I _____ (not/want) to walk the dog, but I went. What a terrible birthday!

I _____ (get back) at about 5 o'clock. While I _____ _____ (walk) upstairs, my mum called, "I _____ (wash) your clothes but there are some more on your bed." I went downstairs again and into the living room. It was full. All my friends and my family _____ _____ (wait) for me. It was a surprise party. "I _____ (not/believe) it," I said. "This only _____ (happen) in books."

Kommunikationsübung

7 In London. Formuliere mithilfe der Anweisungen, was du sagen würdest. Höre dann auf der CD, ob du richtig liegst. Höre sie ein zweites Mal an und sprich dann deinen Rollenteil nach.

At an underground station

(Grüße und frage, wie viel eine Netzkarte kostet:)

You: _____

Ticket office: It's three pounds eighty.

(Frage, ob es einen besonderen Tarif für Kinder gibt:)

You: _____

Ticket office: Yes, it's one pound ninety.

(Sage, dass du eine Netzkarte für Kinder haben möchtest:)

You: _____

Ticket office: Here you are.

In a café

(Mach den Kellner auf dich aufmerksam und frage nach der Speisekarte:)

You: _____

Waiter: Yes, of course.

(Der Kellner bringt sie. Bedanke dich und frage, was das Tagesessen ist:)

You: _____

Waiter: It's spaghetti with fresh vegetables.

(Sage, dass du zwei Tagesessen haben möchtest:)

You: _____

Revision A | **Rückblick** | **Ausblick**

Hörverstehen 🎧 18

8 Patrick trifft sich nach seinem Ferien in London mit Caroline. Höre dir den Dialog an, dann beantworte die Fragen mit *right* oder *wrong*.

1. They both think London is the most exciting city in Britain. _____
2. Patrick thinks you get the best views from the London Eye. _____
3. He thinks Canary Wharf is more interesting than Covent Garden. _____
4. Patrick's uncle lives in Canary Wharf. _____
5. Patrick met Emma at Covent Garden. _____
6. Emma was visiting her uncle in London. _____

Schreiben

9 Schau dir das Bild an und beschreibe, was die Schüler und Schülerinnen gerade tun und was sie am Wochenende machen werden.

_____
_____
_____
_____
_____

Unit 4

Musik und Stars

1 Löse den Buchstabensalat auf und ordne die Wörter richtig zu.

shafion dolme – yob badn – mage wosh – ginless schrat – milf rats – gingins sonless

1. You need these if you want to be a good singer. _____
2. You must be tall if you want to be one of these. _____
3. You can win money or other things on one of these. _____
4. You can listen to this every week on the radio. _____
5. You must be a very good actor to be one of these. _____
6. A group of boys or young men who make music. _____

Wichtige Wendungen

2 Verbinde die Satzhälften zu sinnvollen Sätzen.

Last year I joined	for a picnic after we've practiced next time.
I must give	much money.
We're going to go	a presentation about the band at school.
We're going to do	photos.
Most singers don't make	fun.
It's more important to have	the shopping for the picnic after school.
I'm going to take	a band.

Rechtschreibung

3 Finde die neun Schreibfehler im Text und korrigiere die Wörter.

I want to be a filmstar,

And have a racing car.

I want to be an acter

and go to parties after

every film I make

is that a big mistaik?

I want to be a dancer

or maybe a football plaer

who scores with every shott

and goes to parties a lot.

I'd like to be a drumer

or maybe a famous singer

at the top of the chearts

breaking fans' hearts

but I'm not a great sucess

at singing and all the rest.

But at one thing I'm the best,

I'm the greatest speler! Yes!

Wortschatz 4

Verben

4 Finde die neun Verben im Wortgitter. Tipp: Ein Verb besteht aus zwei Wörtern.

T	E	A	S	E	J	P	U	S	H
R	D	U	I	X	A	K	E	C	K
A	Q	D	V	D	Y	E	T	O	Q
I	Y	I	E	N	D	F	Z	R	D
N	N	T	R	F	G	K	U	E	S
M	G	I	V	E	U	P	A	S	J
P	T	O	B	E	L	B	L	S	H
U	Z	N	A	L	O	J	O	I	N

5 Trage die Verben aus Aufgabe 4 in der richtigen Zeitform in die Lücken ein.

If you want a part in a play, you must usually _____.

Football players usually _____ for a few hours every day.

I _____ an orchestra when I was ten.

I _____ really nervous when I first auditioned.

I _____ my first goal yesterday. It was great.

My parents have never _____ me but they've always helped me.

My friends often _____ me now that they can see me on TV.

It was difficult at first but I never _____.

I _____ my hair when I joined the band.

69

Das unregelmäßige Partizip Perfekt

6 *Have you ever …?* Ergänze die richtige Form der angegebenen Verben.

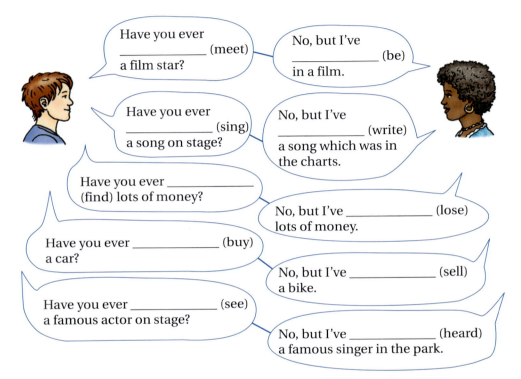

Have you ever _____ (meet) a film star?

No, but I've _____ (be) in a film.

Have you ever _____ (sing) a song on stage?

No, but I've _____ (write) a song which was in the charts.

Have you ever _____ (find) lots of money?

No, but I've _____ (lose) lots of money.

Have you ever _____ (buy) a car?

No, but I've _____ (sell) a bike.

Have you ever _____ (see) a famous actor on stage?

No, but I've _____ (heard) a famous singer in the park.

Signalwörter

7 Trage das richtige Signalwort ein.

never   **yet**   **ever**   **so far**

Have you _____ met somebody famous? – No, I've _____ met anybody famous.

Have you made a CD _____ ? – Yes, we've made two _____ .

Grammatik 4

Die einfache Vergangenheit (Wiederholung)

Du verwendest die einfache Vergangenheit, um etwas auszudrücken, das schon passiert oder vorbei ist. Bei Fragen und Verneinungen verwendest du bei Vollverben *did*. Die Form ist bei jeder Person gleich:
What **did you do** yesterday? – I **went** shopping. My friends **didn't come** with me.
Bei Fragen mit *to be* stellst du *was* oder *were* vor das Subjekt:
Where **were you** this morning? You **weren't** in school. – I **was** at home. – **Were you** ill? – Yes, I **was**.

8 Mike wird berühmt. Ergänze in dem Dialog die richtige Form der Verben.

Paul: _____ (you/watch) that singing competition on TV last night?

Mike: No, _____ (short answer). _____ (be/it) good?

Paul: No, _____ (short answer). The singers _____ (be) terrible. Nobody's going to become a star. So what _____ _____ (you/do)?

Mike: I _____ (go) to the theatre.

Paul: You _____ (not/watch) a play, _____ _____ (question tag)?

Mike: No, _____ (short answer). I _____ (audition) for a part in a play.

Paul: _____ (you/get) it?

Mike: Yes, _____ (short answer).

Paul: Wow. So you're going to become a star.

Das Perfekt: regelmäßige und unregelmäßige Formen

Du verwendest das *present perfect*, um auszudrücken, dass etwas passiert ist und eine Auswirkung auf die Gegenwart hat:
Dad **has bought** a new car. → Wir haben es immer noch.
Oder man verwendet es, wenn etwas gerade passiert ist:
John and Chris **have just had** lunch.
Man verwendet **have** mit *I, you, we, they* und **has** mit *she, he, it*.

Handlung:	Wirkung/Ergebnis:
Bill **has found** some money.	→ He has got it now.
We**'ve been** to Italy.	→ We know what Italy is like.
I **haven't eaten**.	→ I am hungry.
She **hasn't arrived** yet.	→ She is not here.

9 Schauspielern. Bilde ganze Sätze im Perfekt.

John – to act – not – on stage

_____

he – to practise – really hard for the play

_____

I – just – to watch – the play

_____

I – to see – not – a better actor

_____

10 Vor der Aufführung. Übersetze.

John ist gerade im Theater angekommen. Er fühlte sich den ganzen Tag nervös.

_____

_____

Grammatik 4

Das Partizip Perfekt

Das *past participle* ist die dritte Verbform. Du verwendest es, um das *present perfect* zu bilden.

infinitive	simple past	past participle	
to laugh	laugh**ed**	laugh**ed**	**regular:** Du bildest das Partizip Perfekt genau wie das *simple past.*
to smile	smil**ed**	smil**ed**	
to try	tr**ied**	tr**ied**	
to see	saw	**seen**	**irregular:** Diese Formen musst du lernen. Manchmal sind sie wie das *simple past,* manchmal nicht.
to write	wrote	**written**	
to sing	sang	**sung**	
to sell	sold	**sold**	

11 Vervollständige die Tabelle.

kaufen	_____	_____	_____
_____	to fall	_____	_____
_____	_____	heard	_____
_____	_____	_____	read
sehen	_____	_____	_____

12 Kurze Liebe. Ergänze die richtige Form der Verben aus Aufgabe 11.

Jane has _____ a great song on the radio and so she's just _____ a new CD. Jane's at home now and she's just _____ a picture of the singer, and she's _____ in love with him. He's very good-looking. It's evening now and Jane's in the living room. She's just _____ an interview with the singer in a magazine. "What a silly man!" she thinks. She's not in love with him now.

Das Perfekt: Fragen und Kurzantworten

Bei Fragen steht vor dem Subjekt *have* oder *has*. Kurzantworten bildest du ebenfalls mit *have* oder *has*:

Have you eaten yet? — Yes, I have.
Has Dad got home? — Yes, he has.
Has he cooked dinner? — No, he hasn't.
Have Mum and Dad bought some food? — Yes, they have.
What have you done today? — I've visited Grandma.

Im Englischen steht das *past participle* immer **vor** dem Objekt.

13 Baue aus den angegebenen Wörtern Fragen und Antworten.

A: stage – have – a – you – ever – song – sung – on – ?

_____

B: no, – sung – I – I've – haven't, – but – bathroom – lots – songs – in – of – the

_____

A: practised – how – competition – has – Phil – the – for – ?

_____

B: his – him – have – friends – helped

_____

A: ever – has – acted – Tina – in – on – a – play – TV – ?

_____

B: yet – been – she – has – on – not – TV

_____
_____

74

14 Ein Interview mit Steve, einem Fußballspieler. Trage die richtige Form des Perfekts ein.

Ann: United's manager _____ (ask) you to play in their first team. How do you feel?

Steve: It's a dream. I _____ (be) a United fan all my life.

Ann: You've got an important match on Saturday. _____ (you/play) with United before?

Steve: No, _____, but I _____ (train) with them, of course.

Ann: You _____ (not/finish) school yet. How _____ (you/practise) with United?

Steve: I _____ (practise) with them every morning and I _____ (have) special lessons in the afternoon or evening.

Ann: _____ (the manager/give) you some tips for the game?

Steve: No, _____. I _____ (not/speak) to him yet but the team's going to meet tomorrow morning.

15 Übersetze.

Hast du jemals einen bekannten Menschen getroffen? – Ja. Ich habe ein paar Mal mit einem bekannten Schauspieler geredet. Er hat mir aber nie geantwortet.

_____

_____

_____

Signalwörter für das Perfekt

Um zu wissen, ob du das Perfekt verwenden musst, achte auf Signalwörter. Sie erklären dir, wann die Handlung passiert ist und wie oder ob sie mit der Gegenwart zusammenhängt.

John has scored twenty goals **so far** this year.	bis jetzt
Have we **ever** played a match against this team?	jemals
John has **never** played against them.	(noch) nie
I've **just** arrived at the game.	gerade eben
The game has **already** started. (Aussage)	schon
Has anybody scored **yet**? (Frage/Verneinung)	schon
No, **no**body has scored **yet**. (Aussage)	noch nicht

16 Baue aus den Satzbestandteilen vollständige Sätze.

ever – have – fallen – you – in – love – ?

_____

yet – you – have – bought – of – your favourite – a poster – pop star – ?

_____

already – two – I've – letters – to – written – him

_____

17 Fragen an ein neues Bandmitglied. Ergänze die passenden Signalwörter.

– Have you _____ sung in a band?

+ No, I've _____ sung in a band but I've _____ sung on

stage four times.

– Have you made any singles _____?

+ Yes, I've made two _____ but nobody has bought

them _____. And I've _____ written two new songs.

Grammatik 4

Das Perfekt und die einfache Form der Vergangenheit

Wie der Name schon sagt, verwendest du das **present perfect**, wenn eine Handlung etwas mit dem *present*, also der Gegenwart zu tun hat: Die Auswirkung ist immer noch spürbar:
I**'ve never met** your sister. → Ich weiß nicht, wie sie ist.
He**'s eaten** too much. → Er fühlt sich immer noch schlecht.
I**'ve** never **been** to London. → Bis jetzt war ich nicht dort.

Verwende das **simple past**, wenn du sagen willst, wann in der Vergangenheit etwas passiert ist:
I **met** Tom yesterday.
John **ate** too much last week.
Aufgepasst: Das deutsche Perfekt entspricht nicht immer dem englischen *present perfect*:
Yesterday I **bought** a book. = Gestern **habe** ich ein Buch **gekauft**.
Versuche also nicht direkt zu übersetzen, sondern schaue dir immer erst die Signalwörter an:
present perfect: never, ever, so far, already, yet, just
simple past: yesterday, in (2006), (a few days) ago, when, last (week)

Zuhören und verstehen 19

18 Höre zu. Sind die Kurzgespräche im Perfekt oder in der einfachen Form der Vergangenheit? Welches Signalwort wird verwendet?

	Signalwort	present perfect	simple past
1.	_____	☐	☐
2.	_____	☐	☐
3.	_____	☐	☐
4.	_____	☐	☐
5.	_____	☐	☐
6.	_____	☐	☐

19 Rob unterhält sich mit Liz. Ergänze die richtige Form des Verbs.

Rob: _____ (you/ever/be) on TV, Liz?

Liz: Yes, I _____ (be) in two game shows so far.

Rob: Really? When _____ (you/be) in a game show then?

Liz: Well, last week I _____ (be) in a spelling competition.

Rob: _____ (you/win) anything?

Liz: Yes, I _____ (win) some money, but I _____

_____ (already/spend) it.

20 Ein Gespräch mit einem Tänzer. Übersetze.

Wie viele Wettbewerbe hast du schon gewonnen?

_____

Ich habe bis jetzt zwei gewonnen.

_____

Toll. Und hast du jemals mit einer bekannten Tänzerin getanzt?

_____

Ja. Letzte Woche habe ich mit einem Weltchampion getanzt.

_____

Und war es besser als vorher?

_____

Ja, es war viel leichter. Und es hat sehr viel Spaß gemacht.

_____

Das Wesentliche verstehen

21 Anna und Jim schreiben einander E-Mails. Jim ist gerade nach London gezogen, um eine Theaterschule zu besuchen. Welche E-Mail wurde wann von wem geschrieben?

A: I love it here in London. You must come here, too – you're so good at dancing. We've had dancing lessons, singing lessons and Maths and English, of course – yuk! The other kids are really nice and we've all been on a tour of London together. Good luck with the musical and come and visit me soon.

B: I got the part in the film but I didn't take it. I've given up drama school and I'm going to come home. I didn't like the people at school in the end. They're only interested in success and I'm not – now. I don't want to be a star now. I just want to have a normal life. Hope you've got some time for me when I come home.

C: How are things in London? Everything's the same as usual here. School is terrible and the dancing school is great. And guess what! I've auditioned for a part in a musical. They need a 13-year-old dancer and not a singer – lucky for me. Oh, and there's a new boy in our dancing school and he's horrible. He thinks he's so good!

D: It's great that you got the part. Don't worry about the people. Sometimes people get nicer when you know them better. And guess what! I've auditioned, too. For a part in a TV film. And I'm really excited. Drama school's still OK but it's not as much fun as when we started.

E: We've done the play three times now and it's great. I'm still nervous every time I go on stage but I love it when everybody claps at the end. Oh, and do you remember that I told you about that boy from the dancing class? I said he was horrible. Well, he's not, he's really nice. Yes, I've fallen in love with him! I think he was just shy at the start. Good luck with the film and remember me when you get famous!

F: I've got the part in the musical but I'm not sure I want it now. We've practised together a few times and the people are NOT nice. They shout at me when I do something wrong – and that's just the actors! That new boy from the dancing school has got a part in the musical, too, and he's not got any nicer!!

→ Anna's e-mails: first: __C__   second: _____   third: _____

→ Jim's e-mails: first: _____   second: _____   third: _____

4 | Wortschatz | Grammatik | Leseverstehen | Hörverstehen

Einzelheiten verstehen

22 Lies das Interview mit Daniel Radcliffe und beantworte die Fragen mit *wrong* oder *right*.

Interviewer: So you're 17 now and you've already made four Harry Potter films. I think you're the most famous teenager in the world and maybe the richest. How do you feel?
Daniel: Well, it's not easy. I can't always do what I want to do because lots of people are just waiting to take a photo of me and sell it to a magazine. But then I've also really enjoyed making the films, too, so I'm happy I've made them. And the money's great, too. It's nice because I needn't worry about school or jobs.
Interviewer: Do you still go to school?
Daniel: Well, I don't really go to school. Teachers come to me. It's funny because I wasn't very good at school – that's why I auditioned for the first time – but now there are some subjects I love.
Interviewer: Which subjects do you love?
Daniel: I love English and my teacher has really helped me there.
Interviewer: So you're 17. You've made films and even done plays in the theatre. You've travelled the world. You've done many things that lots of people can never do, but do you think you've missed *(vermissen)* something, too?
Daniel: I don't know. How can you know? All I know is that I've really enjoyed the last few years and that I'm really enjoying life now. I've also made some good friends. What more can you want or expect?

1. People all over the world know Daniel Radcliffe. _____
2. Daniel can do what he wants because he has enough money. _____
3. Daniel is still doing school subjects. _____
4. He auditioned for one part because he was bad at school. _____
5. Daniel hasn't acted on stage. _____
6. Daniel has visited many places in many countries. _____
7. He isn't really happy now. _____

Hörverstehen 4

Zuhören und zuordnen 🎧 20

23 Höre dir die CD an und entscheide, welcher Satz gesprochen wurde.

1. a. I've had lunch. ☐
   b. I had lunch. ☐

2. a. She's won the match. ☐
   b. She won the match. ☐

3. a. We've bought some new CDs. ☐
   b. We bought some new CDs. ☐

Zuhören 🎧 21

24 Ein Vortrag. Schau dir die Sätze an. In welcher Reihenfolge würdest du sie in einer Präsentation zu hören erwarten? Höre dann die CD an und überprüfe deine Antworten. Tipp: Es gibt zwei Sätze, die nicht dazupassen.

☐ We hope you enjoyed our presentation.

☐ First, we'd like to say a few words about … and then …

☐ Have you got any questions?

☐ Let's work together.

☐ If you have any questions, we can answer them after our presentation.

☐ Here's a list of …

☐ And finally we're going to …

☐ Our presentation is about …

☐ Who's going to talk about …?

4 | Wortschatz | Grammatik | Leseverstehen | Hörverstehen

Zuhören und verstehen 🎧 22

25 Sieh dir das Bild genau an, dann höre dir die Telefongespräche dazu an. Man hört immer nur einen der Gesprächspartner. Welche der Personen in dem Bild sprechen?

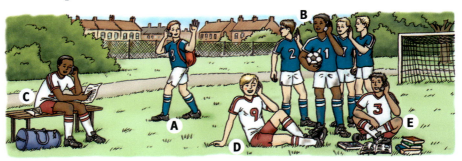

1. _____   2. _____   3. _____

26 Höre dir die drei Gespräche aus Aufgabe 25 nochmals an und beantworte dann diese Fragen auf Englisch.

1. Has he played football today? _____

   What's he going to do in September? _____

   _____

2. How does he feel today and why? _____

   _____

3. What's he going to do this evening and why? _____

   _____

   _____

Unit 5

Sport

1 Finde im Wortgitter sechs Sportarten und schreibe sie heraus. Tipp: Eine Sportart besteht aus zwei, eine aus drei Wörtern.

R	P	W	A	N	W	E	T	R	P	I	W	E
O	R	I	E	N	T	E	E	R	I	N	G	R
E	K	Q	R	A	U	O	W	E	L	D	F	T
J	U	D	O	D	S	U	R	F	I	N	G	E
O	L	D	B	L	D	K	J	L	M	B	A	Q
I	N	L	I	N	E	S	K	A	T	I	N	G
G	R	O	C	K	C	L	I	M	B	I	N	G
U	C	V	S	F	D	J	H	W	A	E	T	K

2 Ergänze die passende Sportart aus Aufgabe 1 mit dem richtigen Verb: *go* oder *do*?

When you _____ _____, you must run and read a map.

When you _____ _____, you usually go to the hills but you can also use a wall in a sports centre.

I _____ _____ because I want to keep fit.

I _____ _____ because it's fun and you must be quick. It's not about fights.

I _____ _____ in a park. It's dangerous on the road.

I always _____ _____ in the sea on holiday.

5 | Wortschatz | Grammatik | Leseverstehen | Hörverstehen

Was man beim Sport braucht

3 Löse die Worträtsel auf und ordne die Wörter der richtigen Beschreibung zu.

roakan   ancoe   pacomss   menpiquet   file-ekjcta

1. This always points to the north. _____

2. You wear this when it rains. _____

3. For some sports you need this and some you don't. _____

4. You can go down a river in one of these. _____

5. You should wear one of these when you're in a boat. _____

Gesundheit

4 Übersetze die gefragten Wörter und trage sie waagrecht in das Gitter ein. Die Buchstaben in den blauen Feldern ergeben das Lösungswort.

Kopfschmerz
Rezept
Schmerz
Tablette
Gesundheit
Krankenhaus
Unfall
Fitness

Lösungswort: _____

Wortschatz 5

Menschen

5 Wer wird hier beschrieben?

1. A person who moves in the water like a fish.   s_____
2. A person who likes books.   r_____
3. A person who writes articles.   r_____
4. A person who helps you get better at sport.   t_____
5. A person who hits other people.   b_____
6. A person who writes prescriptions.   d_____

Der Körper

6 Beschrifte die beiden Bilder.

1.

2.

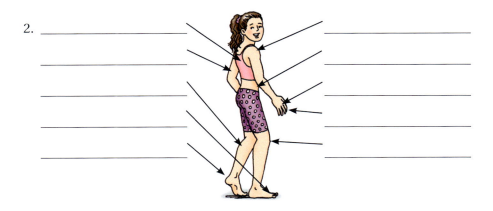

Adjektive: Menschen beschreiben

7 Finde für diese deutschen Wörter die englische Übersetzung.

gesund	h _ _ _ _ _ _
verärgert	a _ _ _ _
übergewichtig	o _ _ _ _ _ _ _ _ _
schnell	q _ _ _ _
schwer	h _ _ _ _
krank	s _ _ _
nass	w _ _

Verben: fit bleiben

8 Wähle das passende Verb und ergänze es in der richtigen Form.

bump into   **keep fit**   **examine**   **weigh**   **jog**   **hit**   **bleed**

Every morning I _____ for an hour because I want to _____. I like food and I eat a lot but I don't _____ too much because I run so often. It's great.

I usually feel really good in the morning but one morning I was jogging and I _____ a tree, fell and then _____ my head on something. It _____ so much that I had to go to hospital. The doctor _____ me and asked, "So what were you doing?" I told him and he said, "Yes, sport isn't always healthy, is it?"

Die Fragewörter *who*, *what* und *which*

Bisher hast du **who**, **what** und **which** als **Objekt** eines Fragesatzes verwendet:

Objekt	Hilfsverb	Subjekt		
What	have	you	eaten today?	was?
Which	does	he	like best – salad or cake?	was (von beidem)?
Who	did	you	invite to your party?	wen?
Who	did	she	help today?	wem?

Du kannst diese Fragewörter aber auch als **Subjekt** des Fragesatzes verwenden. Hier brauchst du **kein Hilfsverb**, um eine Frage zu bauen:

Subjekt		
Who	called you this morning?	wer?
What	helps you keep fit?	was?
Which	makes you happier – food or sport?	was (von beidem)?

9 Eine Umfrage zum Essen. Schau dir die Fragen an: Ist das Fragewort *subject* oder *object* des Satzes?

1. Who do you eat with? _____
2. What did you eat yesterday? _____
3. Who cooks your food? _____
4. What do you usually eat for breakfast? _____
5. Which is healthier – apples or chips? _____
6. What makes people overweight? _____
7. Which do you like best – breakfast or lunch? _____
8. Who is a better cook – your mum or your dad? _____

Wortschatz | Grammatik | Leseverstehen | Hörverstehen

10 Fragen über Fragen. Baue Sätze aus den angegebenen Wörtern.

you – evening – the – What – do – do – in – ?

_____

TV or sport. do – you – best – Which – like – ?

TV or sport.

helps – have – Who – when – you – you – a – problem – ?

_____

you – What – happy – makes – ?

_____

Who – after – do – look – you – ?

_____

11 Ein Gespräch mit einem Koch. Formuliere zu seinen Antworten die passenden Fragen, indem du nach dem unterstrichenen Teil der Antwort fragst.

– _____ at home usually?

+ <u>I</u> usually cook.

– _____ to cook most?

+ I like to cook <u>vegetables and fish</u>.

– _____ healthier – chips or salads?

+ <u>They</u> are both fine, but you mustn't eat too much of anything.

– _____ to cook for?

+ I'd like to cook for <u>children</u> who have only ever eaten fish and chips.

Fragen mit Fragewörtern und Präpositionen

> Viele Verben im Englischen werden mit Präpositionen benutzt. Verb und Präposition bleiben normalerweise eng zusammen – in Fragen und in Aussagesätzen.
>
> | | |
> |---|---|
> | What were you **looking at?** | Was **schautest** du **an?** |
> | I was **looking at** a new CD. | Ich **schaute** eine neue CD **an.** |
> | Who does Pat **look like?** | Wem **sieht** Pat **ähnlich?** |
> | He **looks like** my dad. | Er **sieht** meinem Vater ähnlich. |
> | Where does he **come from?** | Wo **kommt** er **her?** |
> | He **comes from** London. | Er **kommt aus** London. |
>
> Wenn ein Objekt im Fragesatz steht (außer dem Fragewort), kommt es zwischen Verb und Präposition:
> Where did you **get** those trainers **from?**

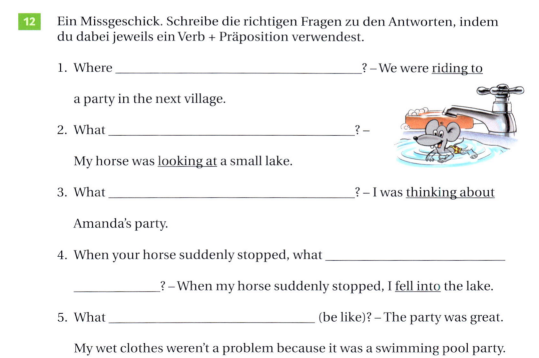

12 Ein Missgeschick. Schreibe die richtigen Fragen zu den Antworten, indem du dabei jeweils ein Verb + Präposition verwendest.

1. Where _____? – We were <u>riding to</u> a party in the next village.

2. What _____? – My horse was <u>looking at</u> a small lake.

3. What _____? – I was <u>thinking about</u> Amanda's party.

4. When your horse suddenly stopped, what _____? – When my horse suddenly stopped, I <u>fell into</u> the lake.

5. What _____ (be like)? – The party was great. My wet clothes weren't a problem because it was a swimming pool party.

Adverbien der Art und Weise

Du verwendest **Adverbien**, wenn du sagen willst, wie jemand etwas macht: He **sings terribly**.
Adjektive verwendest du, wenn du ausdrücken willst, wie jemand oder etwas ist: He's a **terrible singer**.
Adverbien der Art und Weise stehen meistens **nach** Verb + Objekt: He **eats chips quickly**.
Die meisten Adverbien bildest du, indem du **-ly** an das **Adjektiv** hängst. Beachte dabei einige Regeln:

Adjektiv	Adverb	
quick	**quickly**	+ ly (regelmäßig)
careful	**carefully**	-ful → -fully
happy	**happily**	-y (nach Konsonant) → -ily
terrible	**terribly**	-le → -ly

Ausnahmen, die du auswendig lernen musst:

Adjektiv	Adverb
He's a **fast** writer.	He writes **fast**.
She's a **good** singer.	She sings **well**.
They're **hard** workers.	They work **hard**.
I'm **friendly**.	I always talk **in a friendly way**.

13 Schreibe die Sätze mit dem angegebenen Verb neu, indem du jeweils das Adjektiv des Satzes zu einem Adverb machst.

Jean is a happy girl. (laugh) _____

Robert is a quiet boy. (talk) _____

She's a beautiful singer. (sing) _____

He's a terrible actor. (act) _____

She's a good reader. (read) _____

He's a fast runner (run) _____

14 Tennis. Adjektiv oder Adverb? Trage die richtige Wortart ein.

I'm a _____ (good) tennis player but Mathew plays _____ (good), too, and he almost always wins. Last Saturday I really wanted to win. I was _____ (fit) and I was playing _____ (brilliant). The game started _____ (good). Mathew hit the ball _____ (hard) but I was _____ (quick) and I almost always got it back again. After two hours I only needed one more game to win, but I was getting _____ (tired) and Mathew was still playing _____ (beautiful). He won the next game _____ (easy) and my feet were hurting _____ (terrible).

"Oh no, I'm going to lose again," I thought, but then I was very _____ (lucky) – it started raining and we stopped for 20 minutes. That was enough and I won the match. I've never been so _____ (happy) about rain before, but next time we play, I'm going to be fitter.

Adjektiv oder Adverb? 🎧 23

15 Höre dir die Kurzdialoge an. Hörst du ein Adjektiv oder ein Adverb? Trage die Wörter in die richtige Spalte ein.

	Adjektiv	Adverb
1.	_____	_____
2.	_____	_____
3.	_____	_____
4.	_____	_____

Die Steigerung des Adverbs

Wie Adjektive kannst du auch Adverbien steigern. Die Regeln sind die gleichen wie beim Adjektiv.
Adverbien **mit einer Silbe** steigerst du mit *-er* und *-est*:
My mum works **hard**. My dad works **harder**. My grandma works **hardest**.
Adverbien **auf** *-ly* steigerst du mit *more* und *most*:
I'm waiting **excitedly**. My brother's waiting **more excitedly**. My sister's waiting **most excitedly**.
Wie *good* und *bad* sind auch ihre Adverbien unregelmäßig:
good – better – best → **well – better – best**
bad – worse – worst → **badly – worse – worst**

16 Daniel hat zwei Geschwister. Lies die Beschreibungen, dann vervollständige die Sätze mit den passenden Adverbien.

Daniel is fast. Mary is faster and Chris is the fastest.

Daniel runs _____, but Mary runs _____ and Chris

runs _____.

Chris eats healthy food. Daniel eats healthier food. Mary eats the healthiest food.

Chris eats _____, but Daniel eats _____

and Mary eats _____.

Mary is good at football. Daniel is better and Chris is the best at football.

Mary plays football _____, Daniel plays football _____

and Chris plays football _____.

Chris is safe when he's rock climbing. Mary is safer and Daniel is the safest.

Chris climbs _____, but Daniel climbs _____

and Chris climbs _____.

Lesen und einen Bericht schreiben

17 Ein Überfall. Lies die Geschichte und unterstreiche wichtige Punkte. Dann schreibe aus der Sicht von Alan einen Bericht über den Überfall. Achtung: Bevor du anfängst, mach dir Notizen: Was passierte? Wo und wann? Wer war dabei? Verwende die einfache Vergangenheit und achte auf die richtige Reihenfolge.

John Evans is in Year 8 and every Wednesday he goes to computer club so he leaves school late. John lives near school and always walks home. It's the tenth of September today and John is walking past the park. It's about half past four and he's listening to his Discman and so he doesn't hear the three boys behind him. They are sitting in the park when John walks past.
One boy says, "Wow. Look at his Discman. That's a really expensive one. I need a new one."
"Well, let's go and get it," says another and they laugh.
Alan doesn't hear this but he sees the boys come out of the park and walk behind John. Alan goes to John's school but he's in Year 10 and doesn't know John very well. The boys walk behind John and then walk next to him. One boy says, "That's a nice Discman. Can I have it, please?"
John can hear them now and is shocked. He doesn't know what to do. He wants to run but then one of the boys takes his Discman. John shouts, "Give me my Discman back" and tries to get it back again but a boy hits him. He falls on the floor and the boys kick him. He's very scared. He tries to get up again but he can't. Then he hears a voice. It's Alan. Alan sees John on the floor and shouts at the boys.
Alan didn't hear the boys but he saw them hit John and take his Discman. Alan runs to help John and the boys run away. Alan calls the police on his mobile and they arrive after about ten minutes. They take John to hospital but he's OK. Nothing's broken. He's just very shocked.

On Wednesday the 10th of September I _____

_____

_____

_____

_____

_____

Informationen heraussuchen

18 Klettern. Lies die Geschichte und beantworte die Fragen: *right* oder *wrong*?

I've always loved hills and mountains and I've always wanted to climb but I never really had the chance until a new sports centre opened near us and they had a climbing wall. I was so happy. I went climbing every week and loved it but I really wanted to climb in the mountains. After about a year I got my first chance.

Everybody in the rock climbing club drove up to the hills near Manchester and we all stayed in a youth hostel on Friday night. On Saturday we went to a place near a river for our first climb. I looked at the hill and was a little disappointed *(enttäuscht)* because it wasn't very high. I wanted to climb high and look down on the birds. Anyway I started up the hill and it was great. It's different to a wall in a sports centre. It's more interesting and difficult, of course.

I wasn't nervous at all because we all had the right equipment and I knew it wasn't really dangerous. I climbed quite quickly and maybe I wasn't nervous enough because I started taking risks. I took a drink out of my rucksack and it fell from my fingers because I wasn't careful. I looked down. It was the first time that I really looked down and I was suddenly very scared. I couldn't move or think. The bottle broke at the bottom and I'm very lucky that it didn't hit anybody but I didn't think that then. I just hung on to the rope. After some time I heard a voice near me but I couldn't look around.

I don't know how they did it but they got me to the top. When my head became clear, I felt terrible – it was embarrassing, so embarrassing. I never wanted to climb again, but the other climbers were great and the next day I climbed the hill again. I'm older now and I still love climbing. I've climbed many mountains and never had an accident but I never take risks. I know that rock climbing can be dangerous.

1. The first time Max climbed was in the hills near Manchester. _____

2. Max was happy because the hill wasn't high. _____

3. Max wasn't nervous when he started. _____

4. Max's rucksack fell down the hill. _____

5. Max was scared when he looked down. _____

6. Max isn't always careful when he climbs now. _____

Hören und verstehen 🎧 24

19 Beim Arzt. Schau das Bild an, dann lies die Sätze darunter. Welche Personen sagen wohl welche Sätze? Trage die Buchstaben ein. Dann höre dir die Dialoge an. Welche Person spricht in welchem Dialog?

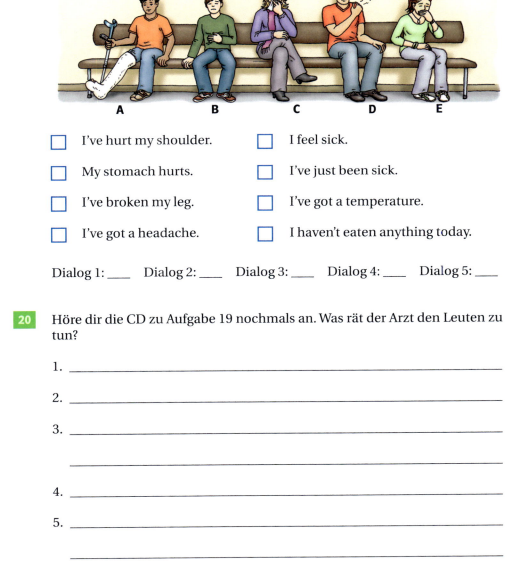

☐ I've hurt my shoulder.   ☐ I feel sick.

☐ My stomach hurts.   ☐ I've just been sick.

☐ I've broken my leg.   ☐ I've got a temperature.

☐ I've got a headache.   ☐ I haven't eaten anything today.

Dialog 1: ___   Dialog 2: ___   Dialog 3: ___   Dialog 4: ___   Dialog 5: ___

20 Höre dir die CD zu Aufgabe 19 nochmals an. Was rät der Arzt den Leuten zu tun?

1. _____

2. _____

3. _____
   _____

4. _____

5. _____
   _____

Hören und zuordnen 25

21 Harte und weiche Konsonanten. Welche Wörter hörst du? Schreibe sie auf.

1. _____ 5. _____ 9. _____

2. _____ 6. _____ 10. _____

3. _____ 7. _____ 11. _____

4. _____ 8. _____ 12. _____

Hören und Informationen heraussuchen 26

22 Ein Interview mit einer Sportlerin. Höre zu, dann beantworte die Fragen.

1. What sport does Liz do? _____

2. How often does she do it? _____

3. When does she do aerobics? _____

4. What does she do on Fridays? _____

5. Is there anything that she doesn't eat? _____

6. When does she read maps? _____

7. Why was it a problem when they almost drove to the south of France?

_____

_____

Revision B (Unit 4–5)

Jobs

1 Finde in der Wortschlange fünf Berufe und die Dinge, die dazugehören, und trage sie in die passenden Sätze ein.

actorchartsdoctorfashionmodelfootballplayerprescriptionmatchsingersuccessuit

A _____ often writes a _____.

A _____ always wants to win the _____.

A _____ wants to be at the top of the _____.

An _____ wants _____.

A _____ must sometimes wear a _____.

Körperteile, Krankheit und Sport

2 Löse die Anagramme auf und ordne die Wörter richtig ein.

berioacs   edheacha   odju   kene
cnek   ortinegiener napi   orck gmilbinc
ckis   mastoch   prateurmeet   eto

parts of your body	health	sport
_____	_____	_____
_____	_____	_____
_____	_____	_____
_____	_____	_____

Verben

3 Verben, die aus zwei Wörtern bestehen. Übersetze.

aufgeben _____ wählen _____

auslachen _____ anlächeln _____

zusammenstoßen _____

4 Löse das Kreuzworträtsel und baue das Lösungswort aus den Buchstaben in den hinterlegten Kästchen zusammen.

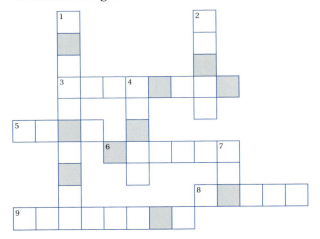

1. When you know what a word means, you … it.
2. When something red comes out of your knee, for example, you …
3. When a doctor looks at somebody, he or she … her or him.
4. When something goes from one place to another, it …
5. If you are not careful, you … an accident.
6. If you tell somebody something that they have forgotten, you … them.
7. When you colour your hair, you … it.
8. I … more than you but I'm not overweight.
9. When you want a part in a play, you must …

Lösungswort (zwei Wörter):

When you explain yourself, you g___ _____.

Das Perfekt und die einfache Vergangenheit

5 Bilde vollständige Sätze und Fragen in der richtigen Zeitform.

you – ever – to play a trick on – your English teacher – ?

_____

what – you – to do – yesterday – ?

_____

I – never – to climb – a mountain

_____

6 Ergänze die in Klammern angegebenen Verben in der richtigen Zeitform.

I _____ (never/be) on stage but I've always wanted to act in a play. My problem is that I _____ (always/be) nervous. A few weeks ago I _____ (see) a poster. It said that they were looking for young actors for a play. I wanted to go but I _____ _____ (not/think) that I could. I _____ (know) that people from my school wanted to audition and I'm always more nervous when I know people. Then I had a brilliant idea. I _____ (dye) my hair and wore sunglasses. It worked. I _____ (feel) really cool with the sunglasses and I auditioned really well. Then as I _____ (leave) the theatre, John, a boy from my school shouted, "Cool sunglasses, Nick!" How embarrassing! But it wasn't a problem. I _____ (already/hear) from the theatre and yes! I've got the part.

Übersetzung

7 Ein Interview mit einem Schauspieler. Übersetze.

Cinema News: Hi Sasha. Es ist toll, dass du hier bist.
Sasha Darnell: Vielen Dank. Ich freue mich, hier zu sein.
Cinema News: Ich würde dir gern Fragen über dein Leben stellen. Wie wurdest du Schauspieler?
Sasha Darnell: Na ja, es fing in der Schule an. Ich war nicht sehr gut in der Schule, aber wenn ich witzige Sachen machte, lachten die Leute. Das gefiel mir, also spielte ich in der Schule Theater.
Cinema News: Wer hat dir in der Schule geholfen?
Sasha Darnell: Ted Smith. Er ist ein guter Englischlehrer und er kann sehr gut erklären.
Cinema News: Und von wem hast du am meisten gelernt?
Sasha Darnell: Am meisten habe ich von meiner Mutter gelernt. Sie lacht immer, auch wenn es nicht gutgeht.

| Ausblick | Revision B |

Schreiben und Zuhören 🎧 27

8 Schau dir das Bild an. Was kannst du über Emily und Helen herausfinden? Vergleiche die beiden und schreibe auf, was dir auffällt. Verwende dazu die unten angegebenen Wörter. Dann höre dir das Interview mit den beiden an und ergänze bzw. korrigiere, was du geschrieben hast.

fast **beautiful** **win** **become** **tennis lessons**

_____
_____
_____
_____
_____
_____
_____
_____
_____
_____
_____

Unit 6

In Schottland

1 Hobbys. Löse die Buchstabendreher auf und ergänze damit die Sätze.

shgfiin   gapibpes   iclamsu tinsstrunem   hiek   dceiihl

The guitar and the drums are _____.

The _____ are an old Scottish instrument.

At a _____ you dance to old Scottish music.

Lots of people _____ in the Scottish mountains.

Many people go _____ in the Scottish lochs or rivers.

2 Finde in der Wortschlange sechs Begriffe, die mit Arbeit zu tun haben, und schreibe sie an den richtigen Stellen in den Text.

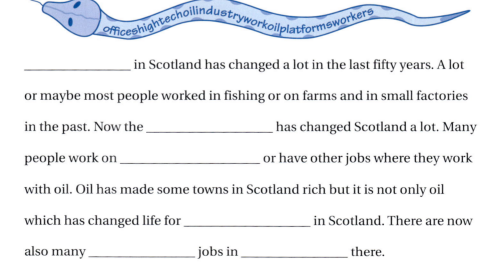

officeshightechoilindustryworkoilplatformsworkers

_____ in Scotland has changed a lot in the last fifty years. A lot or maybe most people worked in fishing or on farms and in small factories in the past. Now the _____ has changed Scotland a lot. Many people work on _____ or have other jobs where they work with oil. Oil has made some towns in Scotland rich but it is not only oil which has changed life for _____ in Scotland. There are now also many _____ jobs in _____ there.

Das Wetter

3 Ergänze die richtigen Wörter.

It's going to _____ tomorrow.

It's often _____ near the coast.

There are often _____ over the hills.

It can be dangerous on an oil platform when there's a _____.

We're going to have a beautiful _____ day tomorrow.

It's difficult to land a helicopter when there's lots of _____.

Freiheitskampf

4 Baue aus den Wortteilen sieben Wörter zusammen und ergänze sie im Text.

bat	sol	ki	he	ene	pris	fou
dier	oner	my	tles	ght	ll	ro

I'm not a _____ but I'm a Scot and I'm fighting so that I can be free. The English steal my land and _____ my sons; I must fight them. I am not a _____ but I have known a few – men who have risked or given their lives for other people although they were scared.

I have _____ many _____ but I'm getting old now and maybe this was my last. I have been caught by my _____.

Will they kill me or just keep me _____? I don't know but I hope the future will be better for the Scots.

Menschen beschreiben

5 Löse das Kreuzworträtsel. Wie lautet das Lösungswort?

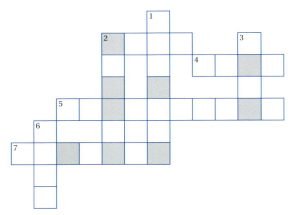

down:
1. If you can try again and again when something doesn't work, then you are …
2. Somebody who is nice, helps other people and doesn't hurt anything is …
3. Somebody who is friendly to other people is …
6. If you are not strong, you are …

across:
2. When you are happy about something, then you are …
4. Somebody who is not overweight is …
5. If you get very angry very quickly, you are …
7. If you never do anything wrong, you are …

Lösungswort: _ n _ _ _ _ s _ _ _ _

Verben

6 Übersetze folgende Verben.

schicken   to s _ _ _   hoffen   to h _ _ _

besitzen   to o _ _   teilen   to s _ _ _ _

versprechen to p _ _ _ _ _ _

Gefühle ausdrücken

7 Wie würdest du dich in den folgenden Situationen fühlen? Löse die Anagramme auf und ordne sie zu.

cextied　　servoun　　yarng　　sda　　dgla

1. It's your birthday tomorrow and you're going to a concert. You're going to meet your favourite star.

2. Somebody has broken your Discman and they didn't tell you. Now you can't listen to your favourite music.

3. You're going to audition for a part in a play later today. You really want the part.

_____　　_____　　_____

4. Your favourite grandma has died. She wasn't very old and you didn't expect it.

5. Your best friends weren't speaking because they both felt angry with the other. They're friends again now.

_____　　_____

Wichtige Ausdrücke: rund ums Postamt

8 Vervollständige die Wendungen.

E _ _ u _ _ m _, _ l _ _ s _. W _ _ r _ _ a _ I _ _ y _ _ a _ _ s? – At that shop over there.

I_ _ h _ _ e a _ _ s _ _ f _ _ c _ _ e _ _ h _ _ e? – Yes, it's opposite the station.

_ _ w _ _ c _ _ s _ _ o _ _ c _ _ d _ o _ _ _ m _ _y? – It's 35p.

W _ _ r _ _ s _ _ e _ _ a _ _ _ t _ _ s _ _ o _, _ l _ _ s _? – It's in front of the newsagent.

_'_ l _ _ e _ _ v _ _ t _ _ p _ _ o _ _ e _ _ a _ _. – Here you are.

105

Die Possessivpronomen

Possessivbegleiter + Nomen	Possessivpronomen
Is that **my** bag?	No, it's **mine**.
Where did you buy **your** bag?	In town. Where did you buy **yours**?
He's lost **his** mobile.	Isn't that **his** on the table?
Is that **her** house?	No, **hers** is next door.
Great. Here is **our** bus.	No, that's not **ours**. We need the 4.
Girls, are these **your** cups?	Or are they **yours** over there?
Is that **their** car?	No, **theirs** is red.

9 Im Café. Ergänze die richtigen Possessivpronomen.

Sue: Look! Here's the waiter with our dinner.

John: No, that's not _____. Look! It's _____. He's going to their table.

Sue: Oh yes. But here is _____. Look, that's our waiter.

John: Thank you. The fish. That's _____. Yes, I ordered that. And the chicken – that's _____, isn't it, Sue?

Sue: No, it's not _____. I ordered chicken with fresh vegetables.

Waiter: Oh, I think, it's _____ over there. He hasn't got his meal yet.

Possessivbegleiter oder Possessivpronomen? 28

10 Vor einer Wanderung. Wird der Possessivbegleiter oder das Possessivpronomen verwendet? Schreibe auf, was du hörst, und bestimme, ob es sich um Begleiter oder Pronomen handelt.

1. _____   4. _____

2. _____   5. _____

3. _____   6. _____

Grammatik 6

Das *Will*-Futur

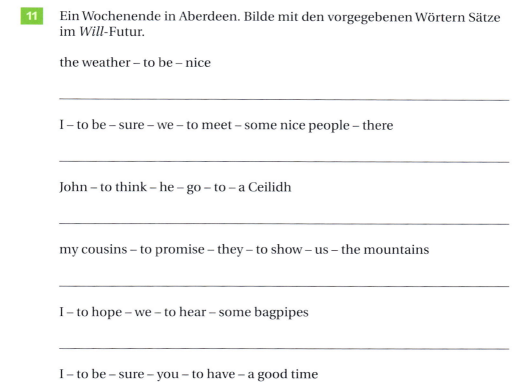

Das *Will*-Futur hat für alle Personen die gleiche Form:
will oder *'ll* + Infinitiv:

I**'ll see** John later.	Ich werde John später sehen./Ich sehe John später.
She **will win** the match.	Sie wird das Spiel gewinnen.
We**'ll have** a good time there.	Wir werden eine gute Zeit haben.

Du verwendest das *Will*-Futur, wenn du über etwas redest, das in der Zukunft passieren wird und worauf du keinen Einfluss hast, z. B.: It'll rain tomorrow. He'll be 17 on Saturday.
Mit *will* verwendest du oft Ausdrücke wie *I think, I'm sure* oder *I hope*, z. B.: I'm sure he'll get here soon.

11 Ein Wochenende in Aberdeen. Bilde mit den vorgegebenen Wörtern Sätze im *Will*-Futur.

the weather – to be – nice

_____

I – to be – sure – we – to meet – some nice people – there

_____

John – to think – he – go – to – a Ceilidh

_____

my cousins – to promise – they – to show – us – the mountains

_____

I – to hope – we – to hear – some bagpipes

_____

I – to be – sure – you – to have – a good time

_____

Die Verneinung des *Will*-Futurs; Fragen mit Kurzantwort

Will the Ceilidh be good? – Yes, it will. It'll be great.
Will you be 12 this year? – No, I won't. I'll be 13.

Wird das Ceilidh gut sein? – Ja. Es wird super.
Wirst du dieses Jahr 12? – Nein. Ich werde 13.

Die Verneinung von *will* bildest du mit *will not* oder *won't*:
I'm sure it **won't** rain tomorrow.
We **will not** be late. We've got lots of time.

12 Urlaub am Loch Ness. Bilde Fragen, Kurzantworten und ergänzende Erklärungen mit dem *Will*-Futur.

1. I – to need – an anorak? – Yes. It – to rain – tomorrow

    _____

    _____

2. we – to see – the Loch Ness Monster? – No. It – not – to want – to talk – to us

    _____

    _____

3. we – to catch – some fish? – Yes. I – to be sure – we – to be lucky

    _____

    _____

4. you – to swim – in – the loch? – No. It – not – to be – warm enough

    _____

    _____

5. Aunt Jane – to visit – us? – No. She – not – to be – in Scotland – next week

    _____

    _____

Grammatik 6

13 Vermutungen über die Zukunft. Übersetze diese Sätze.

Ich glaube, du wirst Schottland verlassen. – Nein. Ich werde Schottland nie verlassen.

_____

_____

Wird John Fußballer? – Nein. Er wird nicht hart genug trainieren.

_____

_____

Werden wir in zehn Jahren Freunde sein? – Nein. Ich werde reich und bekannt sein und dich nicht (mehr) kennen wollen!

_____

_____

_____

Zuhören 29

14 Ein Fußballspiel. Höre zu: Hörst du *we'll, we, won't* oder *don't*? Vervollständige die Lücken.

1. _____ play against Edinburgh on Saturday.

2. _____ play well.

3. You _____ like football.

4. You _____ enjoy the match.

5. _____ win, I know.

Gegenüberstellung: das *Will*-Futur und das *Going-to*-Futur

Man verwendet das *Going-to*-Futur und das *Will*-Futur bei unterschiedlichen Anlässen. Hier ein Überblick:

Das *Going-to*-Futur verwendest du,
– wenn du über einen Plan redest, also wenn jemand etwas vorhat:
– wenn du etwas vorhersehen kannst durch Anzeichen, die es jetzt schon gibt:

I**'m going to meet** Jill next week.
He **isn't going to learn** the bagpipes.
Look! There's not a cloud in the sky. It**'s going to be** a nice day.
We're playing so badly – we**'re going to lose** the game.

Das *Will*-Futur verwendest du,
– wenn du etwas vorhersagen willst, das nicht von einem Plan abhängt:

– wenn du eine Vermutung äußern willst. Dabei benützt du *I'm sure*, *I promise* oder *I think*:

The weather **won't be** good today.
Jack and Chris **will be** 12 on Saturday.
I think you**'ll like** Scotland.
I'm sure she **won't call** us.

15 Aussagen über die Zukunft. Schau dir die Sätze an und überlege, welche Form der Zukunft verwendet wird und warum.

1. Look at that man. He's driving too fast. He's **going to** crash.

2. I think Julie **will** be a television star when she's older.

3. We've decided at last. We're **going to** go to Scotland on holiday.

4. We **won't** need compasses. The signs are very good.

16 Ein Ceilidh. Formuliere Sätze in der richtigen Form der Zukunft. Tipp: Die Sprechabsicht ist angegeben!

What time – you – to get there – ? *(Plan)*

_____

I – to think – we – to leave – home – about – 6 o'clock *(Vermutung)*

<u>I'm not sure.</u>_____

There – to be – lots of people – there – ? *(Vorhersage ohne Plan)*

_____

Yes – all my friends – to go *(Plan)*

_____

17 Ergänze die richtige Zukunftsform des Verbs.

Ben: What _____ (you/do) on Saturday?

Kate: I _____ (go) to Roger's birthday party. _____

_____ (you/go), too?

Ben: No, _____. He hasn't invited me – I forgot to invite him to my

party.

Kate: I'm sure you _____ (get) one. He _____

(be) 16 and he _____ (have) a really big party.

Ben: _____ (he/have) a ceilidh?

Kate: No, _____. He _____ (have) a disco

and I think they _____ (have) some games there, too.

Ben: Oh, that sounds good. I hope he _____ (not/forget) me.

Bedingungssätze in der einfachen Gegenwart

Bedingungssätze bestehen aus einem *if*-Satz und einem Hauptsatz. Im *if*-Satz wird die Bedingung ausgedrückt, im Hauptsatz wird erklärt, was daraufhin passieren wird:
if-**Satz** *(simple present)* **Hauptsatz** *(will future)*
If the weather**'s** nice, we**'ll climb** the mountain.
If you **go** to the Ceilidh, you**'ll meet** some nice people.

Man kann auch zuerst den Hauptsatz schreiben. In diesem Fall brauchst du kein Komma:
We**'ll need** lots of money **if** we go shopping in Edinburgh.

Man kann im Hauptsatz auch ein **Modalverb** oder die **Befehlsform** verwenden:
If you go to Scotland, you **must go** to Loch Lomond. (Modalverb)
If you go into the mountains, **tell** somebody where you are going. (Befehlsform)

18 Ein Besuch in Edinburgh. Verbinde die richtigen Satzteile miteinander.

If we take the first train,	you must visit the castle there.
The shops won't be open	you'll hear some great music.
If you have time,	if a Scot shows you around.
If you like,	if you want to see a lot.
If she has time,	if we get there so early.
Take some good shoes with you	she'll show you around.
You'll see more interesting things	I'll give you my cousin's phone number.
It won't be a problem	we'll get there at 10 o'clock.
If you go to the right places,	if you don't have much money.

19 Zum Ceilidh oder nicht? Trage die Verben in der richtigen Form ein.

1. If I _____ (go) to the Ceilidh, I _____ (see) Kate. I _____

   _____ (be) very happy if I _____ (see) Kate. I _____

   _____ (not/be) happy if she _____ (be) with another boy.

2. Well, she _____ (not/dance) with me if I _____

   (not/ask) her. If I _____ (dance) with her, it _____(be)

   embarrassing – I can't dance. Maybe if I just _____ (talk) to

   her, she _____ (not/want) to dance.

3. If I _____ (have) dancing lessons, I _____ (learn)

   to dance well. If I _____ (ask) her, maybe Kate _____

   (teach) me. If she _____ (teach) me to dance, maybe she

   _____ (want) to go to Ceilidhs every week. Hm! Maybe I _____

   _____ (find) a girl who likes football if I _____ (be) lucky.

20 Die Highlands. Baue aus den Wörtern vollständige Sätze.

go – see – if – you – you – will – lots of – to the Highlands – , – wild animals

_____

must take – want to – climb – you – warm clothes – if – you – the mountains

_____

if – is – it – be – very careful – foggy

_____

if – you – climb – have – a great view – Ben Nevis – , – you – will

_____

Gegenüberstellung: *if* und *when*

If und *when* können im Deutschen beide mit „wenn" übersetzt werden. Im Englischen werden sie aber in verschiedenen Situationen verwendet.
John: **If** I go to Scotland, I'll see my sister. ⟶ **Falls** ich nach Schottland gehe, werde ich meine Schwester sehen.
Hier ist nicht ganz sicher, ob John nach Schottland fährt.
Aber:
John: **When** I go to Scotland, I'll see my sister. ⟶ **Dann, wenn** ich nach Schottland fahre, werde ich meine Schwester sehen.
Hier weiß John sicher, dass er nach Schottland fahren und seine Schwester sehen wird.

21 Loch Ness. Ergänze *when* oder *if*.

Maggie: Oh, did I tell you? We're going to go to Scotland next week on holiday.

William: Oh great. _____ you get there, will you send me a postcard?

Maggie: I'll send you one _____ I can find a postbox. We're going to stay in the Highlands for the first week. Then we're going to stay with my aunt in Inverness and maybe my cousins will be there. _____ they are there, they'll take us to parties.

William: Oh, that's nice. _____ you're there, will you visit Loch Ness?

Maggie: I'm not sure. _____ we've got time, I think we'll go there.

William: Well, _____ you go there, you must look for the Loch Ness Monster. And _____ you see it, you must go to the doctor's right away.

Maggie: Hah hah. Very funny.

Leseverstehen 6

Lesen und Charaktere beschreiben

22 Eine Wanderung im Hochland. Sieh dir die vier Wörter an, die vor dem Text stehen. Was könnte in der Geschichte passieren? Lies dann die Geschichte und finde heraus, ob du Recht hattest. Zuletzt beantworte die Fragen.

mountain   fog   helicopter   hospital

"So where shall we go today?" asked Alan.
"Let's walk along the coast a bit," answered Brian.
"No, that's boring. Let's go up Ben Nevis," said Simon who always got bored easily.
5 "No, the weather's not good enough. It'll be foggy at the top of the mountain and we'll be lucky if we don't get really wet."
"Brian, you're not scared of a bit of water, are you?" said Simon.
"No, but it isn't nice and you know how dangerous it is when it's foggy at the top of mountains," he answered.
10 "Oh, we'll have our compasses with us and our mobiles. What can happen?" said Simon who usually did things first and thought later.
"Yeah, I think we'll be OK," said Alan, "Maybe we'll come out above the clouds and that's fantastic. Maybe we'll even see an eagle *(Adler)*. And we can always come back if the weather gets worse."

15 Three hours later they were all climbing up Ben Nevis. They were climbing through thick fog. It was really cold but it was getting lighter. "We'll see the sun soon," said Alan. He was getting excited. He was a very positive person who loved beautiful places and animals and birds. Then they were through the fog. It was sunny and the sky was a beautiful blue and they could see
20 the top of Ben Nevis not far away. When they looked down, they could only see the tops of the clouds that looked like cotton wool *(Baumwolle)*. It made them all feel very happy and they danced around and almost ran up the mountain. Then they saw an eagle. It flew up from a rock.

"Hey, do you think it's got a nest there?" said Alan.
25 "Let's go and look," said Simon.
"Are you both crazy?" said Brian. "If it's got a nest there, it won't be happy if you go and look at it."
"Oh, we won't go that near," said Alan, climbing up the rock.
"Brian, don't tell me that you're scared of eagles, too," said Simon.
30 They both climbed near to the rock so that they could see the nest and then Alan stopped.
"That's near enough," he said, but Simon didn't stop. He climbed higher and didn't see the eagle behind him.

115

The eagle flew at Simon's head. Simon put an arm up so that he could keep
35 the eagle away but he fell off the rock and landed on Alan.
Simon wasn't hurt but Alan was. He hit his head and didn't open his eyes again.

"Is he dead?" shouted Simon. He was scared now. Brian checked and Alan was OK but his head was bleeding. He tried to use his mobile but, of course,
40 it didn't work up there.
"We must go for help," said Brian. "We must keep Alan warm and one of us must stay here and look after him. Do you want to go?"
"I can't go," said Simon, "My legs are shaking. I can't walk down the mountain now."
45 Brian put his anorak over Alan to keep him warm and walked down again. He hated the fog and he was cold and wet but he stayed very calm. It was only later when the helicopter came and took them all to hospital that Brian's legs shook and he felt sick.

1. Sammle zuerst die Adjektive im Text, die die drei Charaktere beschreiben.

   Alan: _____

   Brian: _____

   Simon: _____

2. Jetzt vergleiche die Charaktere auf Englisch, indem du ihre Aussagen herausschreibst, in denen sich ihre Eigenschaften zeigen. Nimm ein Extrablatt zu Hilfe.

   _____
   _____

3. Überlege, wie sich die Eigenschaften und Gefühle der Charaktere im Lauf der Geschichte auf die Ereignisse auswirken. Schreibe auf einem Extrablatt weiter.

   _____
   _____
   _____

Zuhören 🔊 30

23 In den Ferien. Höre zu und vervollständige die Sätze. Achtung: Manche Wörter klingen gleich, schreiben sich aber unterschiedlich!

I can _____ from my bedroom.

I'm going to go to town _____ a new skirt.

_____ the skirt?

_____ my hair red tomorrow.

_____ sandwiches are _____.

Zuhören und Informationen heraussuchen 🔊 31

24 Höre dir den Dialog an und zeichne die entsprechenden Wettersymbole auf der Karte von Schottland ein. Wo herrscht welches Wetter?

Zuhören und schreiben 🄲 32

25 Nic ist in den Ferien. Höre dir erst das Telefongespräch mit seiner Mutter an, dann vervollständige die Postkarte.

Dear Pete,

We're having a _____

_____. Every day we

_____ in _____ and the weather is _____.

It's _____ and warm every day and we even _____ in

the rivers. Yes, they're very cold but it's _____. Tomorrow we're

_____ Ben Nevis. That will be _____, I think.

In the picture you can see _____. We _____ there on

our first day here and no, we didn't see the monster. Have a good holiday.

CU Nic

Zuhören und das Wesentliche verstehen 🄲 33

26 Bergwandern. Höre dir zunächst den Dialog an, dann beantworte die Fragen.

1. What did they do last night and did they enjoy it?

   _____

   _____

2. What does Jean think they should take up the mountains and why?

   _____

   _____

Unit 7

Mit dem Flugzeug unterwegs

1 Trage die gesuchten Wörter ein.

1. You can fly in a _ _ _ _ _.

2. When you arrive at the airport, you go to the _ _ _ _ _ - _ _.

3. If you want to travel over the sea, you can go by _ _ _ _ _.

4. When you travel from one country to another, you often need to take your _ _ _ _ _ _ _ _ with you.

5. You collect your bags in a _ _ _ _.

6. Your plane maybe late so you must listen for an _ _ _ _ _ _ _ _ _ _ _ _.

7. A _ _ _ _ _ _ _ is a special train that goes between two places.

8. _ _ _ _ _ _ _ is another name for all your bags.

9. If you're meeting somebody who has just landed at the airport, go to _ _ _ _ _ _ _ _.

10. Go to _ _ _ _ _ _ _ _ _ _ _ if you want to fly somewhere.

11. If the weather is very bad, your _ _ _ _ _ _ may be late.

12. When you've got your baggage, you must go through _ _ _ _ _ _ _ _.

13. At some airports there is more than one _ _ _ _ _ _ _ _ _.

Reise nach England

2 Übersetze die Wörter.

Lerner _____   Grammatik _____

Kurs _____   Gastfamilie _____

Unterricht _____   Freunde finden _____

3 Bei einer Gastfamilie. Vervollständige die Lücken mit den passenden Ausdrücken.

What shall I do – Could you lend – Shall I help – Is it OK if – May I have

Yes, of course. I'll get you one.

_____ a glass of water?

Oh, yes, please. That would be nice.

_____ you with the dinner?

Yes, there's one on the bookshelf.

_____ me a map, please?

Oh, give them to me. I'll wash them tomorrow.

_____ with my dirty jeans?

Yes, of course. You can take the phone into your bedroom.

_____ I phone my parents?

Welt und Weltraum

4 Löse die Anagramme auf und übersetze sie.

naile _____ _____

thear _____ _____

queerathak _____ _____

syk _____ _____

panlet _____ _____

Verben

5 Sprachferien. Trage die Verben in der richtigen Form an der passenden Stelle ein.

imagine **improve** **make friends** **take off** **get used to** **miss** **shake**

Last year I wanted to _____ my Spanish and so I went to Spain for a month and did a language course. It was great fun but I had a few problems, too. My first problem was that I hate flying so while we were _____ my legs _____ more than the plane. The second problem was that I _____ my friends at first, but then I _____ with lots of the people on the course and didn't miss my friends at home at all. The third problem was that I couldn't understand anybody because everybody spoke so fast. I _____ that though – after about three and a half weeks! It was my best holiday ever and now I'm home again I can't _____ that I almost didn't go because I was scared!

Die modalen Hilfsverben *may*, *could* und *shall*

Du verwendest **may,** wenn du um etwas bittest. Es ist sehr höflich und formell. In Fragen wird *may* immer mit *I* oder *we* verwendet:
May I use the phone, please? – Yes, of course, you **may.**
Darf ich bitte das Telefon verwenden? – Ja, natürlich.

Du verwendest **could** ebenfalls, um um etwas zu bitten. Es ist ebenfalls höflich, aber nicht ganz so förmlich:
Could I have more chips, please? – Yes, of course.
Könnte ich bitte mehr Pommes haben? – Ja, natürlich.
Could you help me with my bags?
Könntest du mir mit meinen Taschen helfen?

Mit **shall** kannst du einen Vorschlag machen oder fragen, was jemand möchte:
Shall we cook lunch today?
Sollen wir heute Mittagessen kochen?
Shall I lend you my mobile?
Soll ich dir mein Handy leihen?

6 Ankunft bei der Gastfamilie. Bilde aus den angegebenen Wörtern vollständige Sätze.

have – may – please – I – a – glass of water – ?

_____

put – shall – I – my – my – in – bags – room – ?

_____

the language school – where – is – tell – could – you – me – ?

_____

please – garden – look – could – I – at – the – ?

_____

7 In der Sprachschule. Schreibe *may, could* oder *shall* in die Lücken.

Teacher: _____ you all wait over there, please?

Student: _____ I look at your book, please? I've forgotten mine.

    Student 1: _____ I lend you a dictionary?

    Student 2: Yes, please. I haven't got one.

Teacher: _____ I ask you a few questions? I need to know how much you understand.

    Student 1: _____ I help you with those bags? They look very heavy.

    Student 2: Oh, yes, please.

8 Am Flughafen. Übersetze die Sätze.

Darf ich mir Ihren Stift ausleihen?

_____

Soll ich zuerst zum Check-in-Schalter gehen?

_____

Könnten Sie mir sagen, welches Terminal ich brauche?

_____

Was soll ich mit dieser leeren Flasche tun?

_____

_____

Lesefähigkeit: Broschüren lesen

9 Eine Sprachreise. Lies den Text und finde heraus, in welchen Abschnitten du etwas über diese Themen erfahren kannst.

The lessons: _____

Afternoon activities: _____

How old are the students: _____

CANTERBURY School of English

— The best way to learn
In our courses we often speak and we usually listen. We sometimes read and write, but we always have fun. We play games and do role plays and at the end of the course you will have dreams in English!

— Who are the courses for?
We have courses for 13- to 16-year-olds, 17- to 19-year-olds and for 20-year-olds and older.

— How long are the courses?
We have three hours of lessons every morning and we have students from most countries in the world. We have courses that are two weeks long but most of our students stay a month.

— Where can you stay?
Students can choose. You can stay with families or you can stay in rooms next to the school.

— What else can you do?
We organise lots of activities for our students. In the afternoon you can do sports, for example, volleyball, football or table tennis or you can go on trips with other people from your course. There are lots of interesting places to visit in Kent and we usually do a trip into London at the weekend. In the evening you can go to plays or watch films in our own cinema. We also have a disco once a week.

10 Lies den Text nochmals, dann beantworte die Fragen.

1. What do they do most in the lessons? _____

2. How long are the shortest courses? _____

3. What can students do in the afternoons? _____
_____

4. Must students stay with families? _____

Lesen und das Wesentliche verstehen

11 Antonio wohnt bei einer Gastfamilie. Er schreibt seinem amerikanischen Brieffreund. Lies den Brief und stelle die Teile in die richtige Reihenfolge.

A
We watched the football match and we won. It was great in the airport – everybody celebrated – but my dad didn't come back. We waited and waited – an hour and then an hour and a half and he still didn't come. He arrived twenty minutes before my flight and said that he couldn't drive through the streets, because they were full of people in their cars with Italian flags. Anyway I made it and I arrived in Liverpool just two hours late and very tired.

B
My host family met me at the airport and took me to their house, only – you won't believe it – the streets were full of football fans. Liverpool played Manchester and won and all the fans were in the streets and they were all celebrating. My host family were happy because they were Liverpool fans, too, so after about half an hour in the car we got out and celebrated with all the other people. It was great. Nicolas, my host dad, found me an Italian flag and we all sang in the streets. It was the best start you can imagine for a holiday in England. Anyway phone me when you've got time.

C
I don't know how we could forget the football! Anyway after another half an hour my uncle said he would take me. We got to the airport half an hour before the departure of the plane. We ran to departures and they let us go to the front of the queue at the check-in desk so I felt better. But then the woman behind the desk asked me for my passport and I didn't have it.
It was at home in my other bag. I couldn't believe it but then the woman said that the plane was two hours late and I had time to go home and get my passport. It's only 20 minutes to the airport from my house so that was great. My uncle and I waited at the airport and my dad drove my uncle's car to our house.

D
I finally arrived in Liverpool today after an "exciting" trip from Rome. Dad wanted to take me to the airport but when we got in the car, it didn't start. After a few minutes we tried to order a taxi. I said "tried" because no taxi businesses answered the phone. Then we remembered the football match. Italy was playing Germany and all the taxi drivers were watching the football so nobody could take us to the airport.

Richtige Reihenfolge: _____

Zuhören und Einzelheiten verstehen 🔊 34

12 Am Flughafen. Höre dir die Durchsagen an und beantworte die Fragen.

1. Where's the flight going to? _____

   Where do the passengers have to go? _____

2. Where should Emma Walton go? _____

   Who is waiting for her there? _____

3. How long will the flight to London

   Heathrow last? _____

   What time should they get there? _____

   What's the weather like in London? _____

Zuhören 🔊 35

13 Sieh dir die Sätze an. Welche l's oder t's hört man nicht, wenn man den Satz laut liest? Unterstreiche die Buchstaben, dann höre die CD an und überprüfe deine Antworten.

Could you please talk to him for me?

Hey, you mustn't stand on his sand castle.

People are often not very calm at Christmas.

Listen for half an hour to this beautiful CD.

 Wenn du ein neues Wort lernst, sprich es dir ein paar Mal laut vor, um dir die Aussprache einzuprägen.

Hörverstehen | 7

Zuhören und das Wesentliche verstehen 🔊 36

14 Nina aus Deutschland wohnt bei einer Gastfamilie in England. Schau dir das Bild an und überlege, wer die angegebenen Sätze sagen könnte. Dann höre die CD an und überprüfe deine Antworten.

1. Would you like a cup of tea? → _____

2. Could you help me with the dinner? → _____

3. What shall I do with this old newspaper? → _____

4. Shall I lay the table? → _____

5. May I have a cup of tea, please? → _____

Jill   Nina   Bill

15 Schau dir zunächst die Fragen zu dem Dialog in Aufgabe 14 an. Dann höre dir den Dialog nochmals an und beantworte die Fragen.

1. Why does Bill need help with the dinner? _____

_____

2. Does Nina like the tea? Why or why not? _____

_____

Revision C (Unit 6–7)

Reisen

1 Löse die Wortschlange auf und ordne sie der richtigen Spalte zu.

flytraindeparturelandrowrideshipsailflighthelicopterdriveferryplatformroadharbour

	By air	On water	On land
Verbs	_____ _____	_____ _____	_____ _____
Nouns	_____ _____ _____	_____ _____ _____	_____ _____ _____

Adjektive: Menschen und Handlungen beschreiben

2 Welche Adjektive passen am besten zu den in blau gedruckten Aktionen?

gentle – kind – mean – patient – friendly

1. A boy is going home from school and he sees an old lady fall. He helps her home and waits until her daughter arrives. _____
2. A girl had an accident and went to hospital. A doctor examined her and didn't hurt her at all. _____
3. A boy started a new school. He didn't know anybody and he was nervous. A girl talked to him and showed him around. _____
4. A girl was helping her grandma with her shopping. Her grandma stopped and talked to everybody and the girl waited and didn't complain. _____
5. An old man was walking as fast as he could to the bus stop. He just got there when the bus driver drove away. _____

Verben: Sprechen

3 Du kennst inzwischen viele Verben, die mit Sprechen zu tun haben. Löse die Buchstabenrätsel auf und übersetze die Wörter.

skape _____   tearep _____

letl _____   viniet _____

yas _____   houst _____

allc _____   ycr _____

xpanile _____   lkat _____

Adjektiv oder Adverb?

4 Welche Sportart ist die passende für dich? Ergänze die richtige Form der Adjektive oder Adverbien.

The doctor said that I needed to do more sport so I thought very _____ (hard). Which sport was _____ (good) for me? I've always liked football. It's really _____ (exciting) but I can't run very _____ (fast). And rock climbing is even _____ (exciting) but it's also _____ (scary). I'd like to go surfing but I swim _____ (bad). I'm even _____ (bad) at in-line skating. I tried it once and broke my arm. I thought orienteering was fun but it rains too much here and I can't read maps very _____ (good). I thought and thought and then I found the _____ (perfect) sport for me. It's _____ (quick) and fun and you needn't run fast or get wet. It's table football!

129

Einfache Vergangenheit und Perfekt

5 Trage die richtige Form des Verbs ein.

Fiona: I _____ (just/book) an abseiling trip and I'm a little scared. _____ (you/ever/be)?

Steve: No, _____, but I _____ (be) rock climbing and that's almost the same.

Fiona: And _____ (you/like) it?

Steve: Yes, it _____ (be) great fun. It _____ (be/not) scary at all.

Fiona: And why _____ (not/you/do) it again?

Steve: I _____ (have) an accident and _____ (break) my arm.

Fiona: But you _____ (say) it wasn't scary.

Steve: No, it wasn't. I just _____ (fall) over somebody's equipment.

Fiona: And _____ (you/fall) down the mountain?

Steve: No, we _____ (climb) on the wall in the sports hall.

May, could und shall

6 Im Zug. Ergänze *may, could* oder *shall*.

Excuse me. _____ I open a window? It's very warm in here. – Yes, OK.

_____ I help you with your bags? – Oh, that's very nice of you. Thanks.

Excuse me, _____ I sit there, please? – Oh, yes, of course, I'll move my bag.

Die Verlaufsform der Vergangenheit

7 Am Strand. Ergänze die richtige Form der Vergangenheit: Verlaufsform oder nicht?

It was nine o'clock and I _____ (lie) on the beach near my house. It _____ (get) dark and there was nobody else there.

I was looking at the sky when I _____ (see) a bright light.

I _____ (think) it was a plane but I couldn't hear anything, which was strange. The light got nearer and nearer and I _____ (get) very scared when it suddenly went dark.

A moment later the lights were on again and I could see something on the water. It _____ (look) like a big building. While I _____ (try) to get up, a door _____ (open) and some things came out.

I wanted to run away but I couldn't move. They _____ (move) across the water when I heard something.

Were they trying to talk to me? Then I _____ (hear) something that sounded like French and then Russian and then they said in perfect English, "Can you tell us the way to the planet Zarfee, please? We're lost."

Bedingungssätze in der einfachen Gegenwart

8 Der morgige Tag. Schreibe die richtigen Verbformen in den Text.

If it _____ (rain) tomorrow, I _____ (stay) in the house all day. If my mum _____ (have) time, she _____ (bake) a cake. I _____ (not/be) very happy if I _____ (not/get) any letters. If my friends _____ (remember) my birthday, they _____ (visit) me.

Das *Will*-Futur und das *Going-to*-Futur

9 Eine Wanderung. Trage die richtige Form des Futurs ein.

The weather _____ (be) nice tomorrow and so we _____ (hike) by the coast. We _____ (take) our swimming things. I hope the water _____ (not/be) too cold. My mother _____ (meet) us at the end of the walk. I'm sure everybody _____ (have) a great day. I _____ (not/enjoy) it quite as much though, because Ryan _____ (not/come) with us.

Fragen

10 Kennenlernen im Sprachkurs. Bilde Fragen in der richtigen Zeitform.

where – you – come from – ? // you – ever – be – to England – before – ?

_____

who – teach – you – English – ? // what – you – do – next weekend – ?

_____

Besser formulieren

11 Dein erster Tag an der Sprachschule. Verbessere den Text, indem du ihn mit Adjektiven, Adverbien, Ausdrücken der Zeit (z. B. then, next) und Verbindungswörtern (z. B. although, but) flüssiger und interessanter neu schreibst.

Jim, my host dad, wanted to take me to the language school. I went by bus. It was more difficult than I thought. The bus was late. I didn't know where to get off. I couldn't see which stop I was at. I got off at the wrong stop. I didn't know which way to walk. I asked a man. He couldn't speak English very well. He didn't understand the question. I asked a woman. I couldn't understand her. She spoke so fast.
I got my map out of my bag. I was walking down the road. I was looking at the map when I bumped into a girl. She was also reading a map. We both said sorry. We laughed. She was going to the language school. We walked together. She was from Russia. She spoke English badly, too. I couldn't understand her. She couldn't understand me. We had fun. We talked all the way to the language school.

Übersetzung: Beim Arzt

12 Übersetze diesen Dialog.

Arzt: Hallo. Was ist dir denn passiert?
Jenny: Ich bin vom Fahrrad gefallen und habe mich am Kopf und am Arm verletzt.
Arzt: Hast du Kopfweh?
Jenny: Nein, aber mir ist übel.
Arzt: Das ist der Schock. Kannst du deinen Arm bewegen?
Jenny: Ja, aber er tut weh, wenn ich meine Finger bewege.
Arzt: Nun, ich glaube nicht, dass er gebrochen ist. Hier sind ein paar Tabletten gegen den Schmerz. Nimm dreimal am Tag zwei Tabletten.

Doctor: _____
Jenny: _____
Doctor: _____
Jenny: _____
Doctor: _____
Jenny: _____
Doctor: _____

Zuhören und Verstehen 37

13 Packen für die Reise nach England. Höre zu und kreuze die richtigen Kästchen an.

Cecilia packs wellies ☐, an anorak ☐, one pullover ☐, a compass ☐.

In the east of England it's often rainy ☐, foggy ☐, and cold ☐.

Cecilia is going to go orientiering ☐.

Eine Postkarte schreiben

14 Mick verbringt seine Ferien in Schottland. Schau das Bild an und schreibe an Micks Stelle eine Postkarte an seinen Freund Pete. Verwende die angegebenen Signalwörter.

three times yesterday tomorrow

_____

_____

_____

_____

Zuhören: Wichtige Wendungen 🎧 38

15 Verbinde die Fragen mit den passenden Antworten und ordne ihnen die passende Situation zu. Höre dann die CD an und überprüfe deine Antworten.

How much is a travelcard, please?	No, we haven't.	In a clothes shop.
Shall I help you with the dinner?	It's cheese pasta.	Stopping a fight.
Where are the changing rooms?	He hit me.	On the Tube.
Can you tell me what the special is?	No, I don't.	At the doctor's.
Hey, what's the problem?	Over there.	At the post office.
Do you feel sick?	Yes, please.	In a host family.
Have you got any special ones?	5.50.	In a café.

Unit 1

1 register – Namensliste; assembly – Versammlung; break – Pause; planner – Planer/Kalender; timetable – Stundenplan; library – Bibliothek

2

M	A	T	H	S	P	H	B	N
F	R	E	N	C	H	I	M	B
D	E	C	C	I	U	S	O	I
I	S	H	P	E	Q	T	K	O
T	H	N	X	N	E	O	A	L
Z	M	O	W	C	D	R	Q	O
N	L	L	R	E	F	Y	W	G
G	E	O	G	R	A	P	H	Y
O	X	G	E	F	H	E	T	I
P	Q	Y	L	B	C	R	E	U

Maths – Mathematik; French – Französisch; Technology – Computer-Unterricht; P. E. (Physical Education) – Sport; R. E. (Religious Education) – Religion; Science – Naturwissenschaft; Geography – Geographie; Biology – Biologie; History – Geschichte

3
1. I'd like a green door. Can I **paint** it?
2. Those sandwiches look good. Can I **try** one?
3. I often **stay** at my aunt's house in the summer.
4. What time do you usually **arrive** at school?
5. I don't want to **wear** a school uniform.
6. I don't copy her homework but we **compare** our answers.

4 verlieren – to lose
sich rächen – to get your own back
die Anwesenheit kontrollieren – to take the register
überprüfen – to check
(Schulfach) belegen – to take
ausradieren – to rub out
bezahlen – to pay

in Schwierigkeiten geraten – to get into trouble

5 bring – brought; buy – bought; have – had; know – knew; learn – learnt; run – ran; sit – sat; tell – told; wear – wore

6 I **did** my homework yesterday.
I **found** my school books. They were under my bed.
I **saw** a dog at school today. It was in the playground.
My mum **came** to school today. She wanted to talk to my tutor.
I **wrote** a story in French today.
I **went** to assembly this morning.
I **was** late for school today.
I **got** a new planner yesterday.

7 I was late for assembly and then I fell over a chair. It was so **embarrassing.**
My holiday wasn't just good. It was **wonderful.**
Don't be so **negative.** I think it's really good.
I don't like our R.E. teacher. He's too **strict.**
Our homework isn't easy. It's really **hard.**
His parents aren't rich. They're **poor.**

8 I had a great summer. First I painted my room with some green **paint.** It looks interesting. Then we went to Wales on holiday and I tried **abseiling.** That was great and a little scary. Then I went swimming in the sea and saw a **shark.** That wasn't so great and it was very scary.
We stayed on a **campsite.** That was fun and we were lucky because the weather was good all week. A baker lived near the campsite and one day I helped him make some **bread.** The evenings were boring sometimes but one evening we saw a **play** that was really funny.

9 *Gordon:* What **do you do** on Saturday mornings?
Kevin: I **help** my mum in the house or I **meet** some friends.
Gordon: **Does your sister help** your mum, too?
Kevin: **No, she doesn't.** She **works** in my dad's shop.
Gordon: **Does she like** it?
Kevin: Yes, **she does.** Well, my dad **gives** her some money and she likes that. I **don't work** in the shop because my dad says I'm too young.
Gordon: Oh, and what **do you do** on Sunday?
Kevin: We often **go** to the park and my sister often **goes** shopping and buys things with the money from my dad.

10 We **stayed** at home in the summer but the holidays weren't boring. We **painted** our rooms blue, **played** football in the park and **visited** our friends. We often went to London and we **listened** to some good bands in Covent

Lösungen

Garden and we **watched** a play in a park. Yes, our holidays were great.

11
1. On Saturday I stayed at home.
2. My friends visited me in the afternoon.
3. We talked and laughed in the garden until 5 o'clock.

12 We **arrived** at the beach at ten. We **parked** the car and we **carried** our bags to the beach. We **played** football and our dog **chased** some birds. He **tried** to catch one but they were too fast. When we **stopped** for lunch, we saw that the sea was now very near. "It's coming in," **said** my brother. We **finished** our lunch on the wall.

13
[d]: climbed, smiled, tried
[t]: talked, stopped, watched
[ɪd]: needed, painted, started

14 Where were you yesterday lunchtime?
I was in the library.
Were you in the bike sheds at lunchtime?
We weren't at school yesterday.
Chris was in the bike sheds at 12 o'clock.
Your bike wasn't in the bike shed.
It was in your garden.

15 Was Mary in the kitchen? – Yes, she was.
Was Paul in bed? – No, he wasn't.
Were Henry and Liz happy? – Yes, they were.
Were Bill and David in the classroom? – No, they weren't.

16 Were you in assembly this morning? – Yes, I was.
Was it good? – Well, it wasn't interesting, but it was short.

17 I **had** a great holiday in the summer. We **went** to France and we stayed there on a campsite for two weeks. The weather was good and we **did** lots of nice things there. One day I **found** some money. I **told** my sister and she wanted to keep it. I was very good and **told** the woman at the campsite. The next day a man **came** to me and said thank you. He was very nice so I was happy, but the best thing was – I **got** ten euros, too.

18 John learnt a lot last year. [X]
We wear a school uniform at school. [ ]
She bought a postcard at the shop. [X]

19 I didn't ride my bike.

We didn't play football at lunchtime.
John didn't go swimming in the morning.
You didn't laugh at my jokes.
I didn't meet my friends in the afternoon.
We got up late and we didn't go to school.

20 They didn't go swimming.
I didn't play the drums.
The dog chased the cat.
We didn't play computer games.

21
1. Brian didn't go to France.
2. Brian had good weather.
3. Brian didn't stay at a campsite.
4. Brian found a dog.
5. Brian didn't have a good time.

22 Did you all get a new timetable? – Yes, **we did.**
Did Christine arrive late? – No, **she didn't.**
Did the teachers give you lots of homework? – No, **they didn't.**
Did you like your new tutor, Liz? – Yes, **I did.**

23 Did you get a new planner?
Did your teachers give you new books?
Did you listen in assembly?
Did your friends eat all your sandwiches?

24 *Mum:* Did you wash the car?
Lisa: Yes, I did.
Mum: Did you phone Aunt Jean?
Lisa: No, I didn't.
Mum: Did you walk the dog?
Lisa: Yes, I did.
Mum: Did you make a birthday card?
Lisa: No, I didn't.

25 *Paul:* **Did you go** on holiday?
Tina: No, **I didn't. I stayed** at home.
Paul: Oh, but **did you have** a good time?
Tina: Yes, **I did,** but the weather was terrible. It **rained** a lot. **Did you go** away?
Paul: Yes, **I did.** We **went** to Australia.
Tina: Oh great. **Did you like** it?
Paul: Yes, **I did,** but the weather was terrible there, too.

Tina: Really? But it **didn't rain** in Australia!
Paul: Yes, **it did.** It was winter there.

26 *Owen:* Where did you go on holiday?
Zoe: We went to France.
Owen: Who did you go with?
Zoe: I went with my parents, my brothers and a friend.
Owen: How did you go to France?
Zoe: We went by car.
Owen: What did you do there?
Zoe: We went swimming and played on the beach.
Owen: When did you arrive home?
Zoe: We arrived home last night.
Owen: What did you like best?
Zoe: I liked the food.

27 1. wrong; 2. right; 3. right; 4. wrong; 5. wrong; 6. right; 7. right; 8. wrong

28 richtige Reihenfolge: **C – A – D – B**

29 Did you have a nice holiday?
Yes, I did. I had a great time.
Where did you go?
We went to France.
What did you do there?
We visited some friends and we went swimming in the sea.

30 *Chris:* Oh no. I'm late. Where are all my things?
Mum: I don't know. What do you need today?
Chris: Er. My English books and I've got Maths today, I think.
Mum: Well, your books are in your bedroom.
Chris: Oh, and where's my planner? I need my new planner.
Mum: Oh, Chris. Isn't it in your bag?
Chris: Oh, yes. Here it is. Let me see. Oh, of course, I've got P.E., too, and, oh great, History.
Mum: But I didn't think you liked History.
Chris: Yes, I do. We've got a new teacher and she's great.

→ Today is **Thursday.**

31 *Tim:* Hi. Did you have a good summer holiday?
Ellen: No, I didn't. I stayed here and it rained a lot and all my friends were on holiday. It was boring. Did you have a good holiday?
Tim: Yes, I did.
Ellen: Oh good. Where did you go?
Tim: I didn't go away. I stayed here.
Ellen: Oh. What did you do then?
Tim: I worked.
Ellen: Worked? But you're too young.
Tim: No, I'm not. It's work for young people.
Ellen: Oh, maybe I can do that next year. I need some money.
Tim: No, they don't pay you.
Ellen: Oh, so why did you do it?
Tim: Because it was great fun.
Ellen: So what did you do?
Tim: Oh, we painted walls, worked in gardens and went shopping for old people.
Ellen: And that was fun?
Tim: Yes, it was great. Why don't you try it? Or do you think a boring summer is better?

1. right; 2. wrong; 3. right; 4. right; 5. wrong; 6. right; 7. right; 8. wrong

32 *Neil:* I finished three books.
Fiona: I painted the house.
Neil: I walked 20 kilometres.
Fiona: I mended my bike.
Neil: I played football all summer.
Fiona: I visited my cousins in France.
Neil: I watched a few films.
Fiona: It rained a lot.
Neil: I enjoyed my summer holidays.

[d]: played, rained, enjoyed
[t]: finished, walked, watched
[ɪd]: painted, mended, visited

Unit 2

1 The Tate Modern is a famous **gallery.** They have a lot of pictures there.
Buckingham **Palace** is the home of the Royal Family.
The London **Dungeon** is a museum of horror.
You can see a play at one of London's many **theatres.**
When you want to get somewhere, use the **Tube.**
Most tourists go **sightseeing.**
Did you know you can also go **ice skating** in London?

2

q	p	u	k	o	i	b	t
d	i	n	o	s	a	u	r
d	g	z	s	k	j	s	a
k	e	w	q	e	s	k	f
o	o	g	u	i	d	e	f
p	n	y	e	s	g	r	i
c	a	s	e	a	f	m	c
j	k	i	n	g	b	e	n

Three things you can find in a street: traffic, busker, pigeon
Two things you can find in a museum: dinosaur, guide
Two things you can find in a palace: king, queen

3 *Ian:* Let's **take** the Central Line.
Ken: OK. And where **must** we **change** trains?
Ian: At Tottenham Court Road. And we must **get on** a southbound train. Then it's three **stops** to Embankment.
Ken: Must we **get off** at Embankment?
Ian: Yes, we can walk from there.

4 1. passenger; 2. carriages; 3. travelcard; 4. platform; 5. fare;
6. ticket; 7. stop
Lösungswort: escalator

5

infinitive	simple past	German infinitive
to begin	began	beginnen
to catch	caught	nehmen, fangen
to fall	fell	hinfallen
to find out	found out	herausfinden
to fly	flew	fliegen
to hurt	hurt	verletzen
to leave	left	abfahren
to spend	spent	verbringen

6 My day **began** at half past seven and then everything went wrong. I was sitting on a wall and waiting for a new friend in Trafalgar Square when a pigeon **flew** too near me and I **fell**. I **hurt** my hand and **made** my clothes all dirty, so I went to the nearest shop and bought some more. I **spent** an hour in the shop and when I went back to Trafalgar Square, I was late, and my new friend was there. He was talking and laughing with another girl. When the next bus **left** Trafalgar Square, I was on it. Well, my new clothes are nice and the boy wasn't – so maybe it wasn't a bad day.

7 You can write on this: **paper**
This is very old: **antique**
You can eat this and it's often sweet: **fruit**
You should eat one or two of these every day: **vegetable**
You can wear this and it has a good smell – usually: **perfume**
Look at this when you want to know the time: **watch**

8 London is a very **popular** city. Lots of people like it and many tourists go there every year. It's also very **exciting** because there are lots of different people there and you can do so many different things. For example, you can go on the London Eye. It's very **high** and you get a great view of London.
People think that England is always **rainy** but they are wrong. It doesn't rain often in London. It's **true** that there are millions of people in London and the buses and trains are often **full,** but I like that. I think London is the **best** city in England.

9 John **goes** to London every year. He loves it. He always **goes** shopping because he knows some great music shops there, and he always **listens** to the buskers in Covent Garden. This year John is in London again but this year everything is different. It **begins** the same. He **takes** the train to London with his friends and then they go to Covent Garden. They **go** and watch the buskers when suddenly he **sees** a girl he knows from school. The girl**'s playing** a guitar now and she**'s singing**. It's beautiful and lots of people are listening. When she **finishes,** John talks to her. They go and **have** a drink in a café together. They**'re walking** together in Hyde Park now but he **doesn't see** the people there.

10 What **were you doing** at 12 o'clock last night?
I **was reading** a scary book.
My brothers **were looking** for monsters under the bed.
My dad **was working.**
My older sister **was dancing** in a disco.
We **weren't sleeping** but we didn't hear the thieves.
They **were driving** our car away.

11 While the baker's family was sleeping, the fire started.
They were leaving the house when the fire jumped to the next house.
While neighbours were getting water, they lost their houses.
Two days later a large part of London was burning.

12 I was walking though London when I saw Buckingham Palace.
While I was taking a photo, the Queen arrived.
She was walking in the garden when she invited me for a cup of tea.
She showed me her house while we were waiting for the tea.
When I saw the swimming pool, William was swimming in it.
I fell asleep while I was sitting in a living room.
When I woke up, I was sitting at my desk at home.

13
1. He broke his leg while they were playing football./While they were playing football, he broke his leg. – They were playing football when he broke his leg./When he broke his leg, they were playing football.
2. The woman was riding a horse when her mobile rang./When her mobile rang, the woman was riding a horse. – While the woman was riding a horse, her mobile rang.
3. While the man was listening to his radio, he fell asleep./The man fell asleep while he was listening to his radio. – The man was listening to his radio when he fell asleep./When he fell asleep, the man was listening to his radio.

14 I **was travelling** to Covent Garden on the Tube when I **met** a friend. While we **were talking,** the train **stopped** at Covent Garden. The doors **were closing** when my friend **said,** "Didn't you want to get off here?" I got off and the train **was leaving** when I **remembered** that my bag was still on the train. My mobile phone, my money and my travel card were in the bag. I was just thinking, "What can I do now?" when I **saw** another friend. One phone call and ten minutes later I had my bag again.

15

Grundform	Komparativ	Superlativ
little	littler	the littlest
sweet	sweeter	the sweetest
scary	scarier	the scariest
safe	safer	the safest
lucky	luckier	the luckiest
big	bigger	the biggest
good	better	the best

16

Grundform	Komparativ	Superlativ
lucky	luckier	luckiest
big	bigger	biggest
exciting	more exciting	most exciting
beautiful	more beautiful	most beautiful
new	newer	newest
good	better	best
popular	more popular	most popular
happy	happier	happiest
nervous	more nervous	most nervous
bad	worse	worst

17
1. The horse **is bigger than** the pig.
   The pig **is not as big as** the horse.
2. The boy **is as excited as** the girl.
   The chocolate **is more expensive than** the apple.
   The chocolate **is not as expensive as** the sandwiches.
   The sandwiches **are the most** expensive.
3. The computer **is as new as** the bike.

18
Glenda: I love London. It's so much more exciting **than** our town.
Paul: Yes, but it's **more** expensive, too.
Glenda: Oh no. There are lots of shops that aren't as **expensive as** in our town. You can buy some really cheap, cool clothes in London.
Paul: True. And the museums are really **interesting,** too.
Glenda: Yes, they are **the most** interesting museums in England, I think.
Paul: But do you know **the** best thing in London?
Glenda: Er. Covent Garden? The buskers there are really good.
Paul: Yes, they are **better than** the buskers at home. But the best thing is that my favourite football team plays here.

19
1. Graham **is older than** Tina.
   Tina **is not as old as** Janet.
   Graham **is the oldest.**

2. Graham **is not as popular as** Tina.
Janet **is more popular than** Graham.
Janet **is the most popular.**

20 How much are the apples? – The green **ones** or the red **ones?**
Which T-shirt do you want? – The green **one.**
Which bag do want to look at? – The big brown **one.**
How much are those sandwiches? – These cheese **ones** are £1.50.

21 1. The big ones are 30 pence.
2. Would you like to try on this white one?
3. This yellow one?
4. The small one on the wall?
5. Do you mean the blue ones?

22 Do you have a map of London?
She has a nice new T-shirt.
I don't have any money.
London has lots of cheap shops and markets.

23 *Die Sätze 1, 3 und 5 sind nicht mit* have got *möglich.*
2. London's got many stations.
4. I haven't got a ticket.

24 have:
Are you having a good time?
They don't have any good books about London.
We had a great day yesterday.

have got:
She hasn't got any new clothes.
We've got travelcards.
Have you got any information about the museum?

25 *Überschrift:* Interesting places in London
1. Yes, you can.
2. At Madame Tussauds.
3. Yes, it is.
4. At Camden Lock Market.
5. Yes, there are.
6. In Hyde Park.
7. At Madame Tussauds.
8. Yes, you can.

26 Two buskers! – **D**
A day at Covent Garden – **B**
Where can we go? – **A**
Help! I'm not a tourist. – **C**

27 + Excuse me, can you **tell me the way** to the nearest Tube station?
– Yes, go **straight** on and then **take** the first left into Penny Lane.
+ Excuse me, **how** can **I get to** St Paul's?
– **Take** the Northern Line to Bank and **change to the** Central Line. You **need** a westbound train and **it's the first stop.**

28 1.
Boy: OK. We're at Lancaster Gate. So we must take the Central Line to Tottenham Court Road and then change to the Northern Line.
Girl: Yes, and then we need a southbound train and it's just three stops.
→ **Embankment**
2.
Girl: Excuse me, how do I get to …?
Man: Oh, it's a long way. You must go by Tube.
Girl: And where's the nearest Tube station?
Man: Well, Charing Cross is over there. Then you can take the Bakerloo Line to Piccadilly Circus. Get off there and then take the Piccadilly Line. You need a westbound train and then it's only two stops.
Girl: Thank you.
→ **Hyde Park Corner**
3.
Boy: Must we take the Picadilly Line from Green Park?
Girl: Well, we can, but I think it's better to walk to Bond Street and take an eastbound Central Line train. Then we needn't change. And it's only five stops.
→ **St. Paul's**
4.
Boy: Excuse me. How do I get to … by Tube?
Woman: Oh, that's easy. Just take the Bakerloo Line to Piccadilly Circus. Then change to the Piccadilly Line and it's only two stops – the stop after Leicester Square.
Boy: Thank you.
→ **Covent Garden**

29 *Tina:* Was the film good?
Wendy: I didn't see it.
Tina: Why not?
Wendy: Well, you know that I was late this afternoon?
Tina: Yes.

Wendy: Well, I was running to the Tube Station when I fell and hurt my leg. So then I walked to the station but when I got there, there was a big queue at the ticket machine and so I was really late by then.
Tina: So what time did you get to the cinema?
Wendy: At half past three. I was walking up the stairs outside the cinema when they closed the door.
Tina: Oh no. What did you do then?
Wendy: Well, I was just walking around Leicester Square and thinking about what to do when this tourist asked me about Covent Garden. He wanted to go there by Tube and I said it was easier to walk, so I showed him the way. And when I got there, there was some great street theatre and so we both watched for an hour and then he bought me a coffee and …
Tina: So you had a great day?
Wendy: Yes!

1. right; 2. wrong; 3. wrong; 4. right; 5. right; 6. wrong; 7. right; 8. wrong

30 1.
Girl: Oh come on, let's go there. It's the cheapest place and I haven't got any money.
Boy: But it's the most boring, too. What can you do there?
Girl: It's not boring. It's really interesting. You can find out all about science and …
Boy: Wow.
Girl: And there's loads of things you can do there, too.
→ **British Museum**

2.
Boy: Oh. Come on. Let's go. It's great.
Girl: No, we can't. It's so expensive.
Boy: Yes, but it's cheaper than the London Eye.
Girl: Yes, but the art gallery's cheaper and …
Boy: … and more boring.
→ **Madame Tussauds**

3.
Boy: Oh, come on, we have to go. We can't come to London and not go there.
Girl: But it's the most expensive place in London.
Boy: Yes, but it's great and it's open later than the other places you want to go so we can go in the evening.
→ **London Eye**

Unit 3

1 1. **c**ost; 2. changing **r**oom; 3. chang**e**; 4. spen**d**; 5. shopp**i**ng; 6. s**t**yle; 7. po**c**ket; 8. assist**a**nt; 9. **p**rice; 10. cre**d**it
Lösungswort: credit card

2 1. trainers; 2. sweatshirt; 3. shoes; 4. T-shirt; 5. trousers; 6. skirt

3 On Saturday I worked in my dad's shop and **earned** five pounds.
I **lent** Sue five pounds last week but she still hasn't got any money.
Last year I always **spent** too much but this year I'm much better.
I **saved** some money every week last year and now I've got £ 200.
These trainers were expensive. They **cost** £ 35 pounds.
I **borrowed** some money from dad yesterday because I wanted to buy mum a present.

4 stehlen – to steal – stole
werden – to become – became
denken – to think – thought
lesen – to read – read
schütteln – to shake – shook

5 1. He's **mean.** He never spends his money.
2. She's **horrible.** She's never nice to me.
3. He's **aggressive.** He often hits people.
4. She's **greedy.** She always eats too much.
5. He's **popular.** Everybody likes him.

6 Is anybody hungry?
Would you like something to eat?
Can somebody help me, please?
Everything is ready. Come to the table.
I can't find my fork anywhere.
There's nothing on the table.

7 1. glass; 2. fork; 3. knife; 4. spoon; 5. plate; 6. waiter; 7. waitress; 8. menu; 9. dishwasher; 10. fish and chips; 11. burger; 12. salad; 13. meat

8 to lay the table; to clear the table; to wash up

9
- It was your birthday yesterday, wasn't it? What **did you do?**
+ We went to that French restaurant.
- **Did you like** it?
+ Yes, it was great. I love French food.
- **Do you go** there often?
+ Yes, we do. We often go when it's somebody's birthday.
- Who **did you go** with this year?
+ I went with my family and my cousin, Robert, came, too.
- Oh, he lives in France, doesn't he? **Does he visit** you every year on your birthday?
+ No, he doesn't. But his dad's working here this week so he came with him.
- **Does he like** it here?
+ Yes, he does, but he doesn't like the food.

10
You have got some money, haven't you?
They're nice, aren't they?
That isn't expensive, is it?
You bought some new trainers yesterday, didn't you?
You don't like that skirt, do you?
Your dad often gives you money, doesn't he?
We can't have credit cards, can we?
That's really beautiful, isn't it?

11
You can't save money, **can you?**
Rebecca earns some money every week, **doesn't she?**
I'm not mean, **am I?**
You haven't got any money, **have you?**
You borrowed some money from me last week, **didn't you?**
You often borrow money, **don't you?**
Tom's parents bought him a new bike, **didn't they?**
Tom's lucky, **isn't he?**

12
Luca: That looks good, **doesn't it?**
Sophie: Yes, **it does.** But you don't like meat, **do you?**
Luca: No, **I don't.** But it isn't meat, **is it?**
Sophie: Yes, I think, it is. That waiter doesn't want to bring us the menu, **does he?**
Luca: No, **he doesn't.** But we aren't doing anything wrong, **are we?**
Sophie: No, **we aren't.** And we can eat here, **can't we?**
Luca: Yes, if we want to. But we don't want to eat here, **do we?**
Sophie: No, we don't. Let's go.

13 In the kitchen
Dad: It's lunchtime and I'd like **somebody** to lay the table, please.
Pete: Oh, I'm hungry. Is there **anything** tasty for lunch?
Dad: I always make **something** tasty for lunch.

In the living room
Kylie: I want to buy Ginny **something** for her birthday but I can't think of **anything.** Has **anybody** got an idea?
Mum: Look in your magazine. Maybe you can find **something** in there.
Kylie: Has **anybody** got my magazine? I can't find it **anywhere.**
Mum: It must be **somewhere.** You were reading it yesterday.
Pete: Oh, Kylie. Here's your magazine, but there isn't **anything** interesting in it.

14 Would you like **something** to eat? → **Angebot**
Let's go **somewhere** nice on Saturday. → **Vorschlag**
Has **anybody** got my book? → **Frage**
Can you lend me **some** money, please? → **Bitte**
Can I have **some** water, please? → **Bitte**
Can **somebody** help me, please? → **Bitte**
Can **anybody** see my bag? → **Frage**
Can I help you with **something?** → **Angebot**

15 Everybody lends her money.
He finds money everywhere.
I always want to buy everything.

16 1. *Graham:* Can I borrow **some** money, Dad?
    Dad: Why? You don't need **any** money, do you? We buy you **everything.**
2. *Dad:* **Everybody** always wants to borrow money from me.
    Michelle: I don't want to borrow **any** money, Dad. I want you to give me **some.**

17 *Chris:* What did you do at the weekend?
Neil: **Nothing.** It was really boring. There was **nobody** here and I had **nothing** to do.
Chris: Oh, and there was **nothing** on television, was there?
Neil: No, and we have **no** videos.
Chris: So what did you do? You can't do **nothing.**
Neil: No, I did my homework!

3 Lösungen

18 It's difficult to find a present when you've got **no** money and you haven't got **any** ideas. I went to town yesterday and I looked **everywhere** for a present for Angela and I couldn't find **anything.** I asked **everybody** for their ideas but **nobody** had **any.** Then I had an idea. What is it? I'm not telling **anybody.** It's a surprise.

19 1. She's going to pay the bill. – 2. She isn't going to eat a burger. – 3. They aren't going to play a game. – 4. They're going to eat dinner. – 5. He isn't going to clean his room.

20 *Paul:* What **are you going to do** on your birthday, Gemma?
Gemma: **I'm going to have** a party at home. Would you like to come?
Paul: Yes, please. **Are you going to have** it in the garden?
Gemma: Yes, **I am,** if it doesn't rain.
Paul: And **is your sister going to come?**
Gemma: No, **she isn't.** She**'s going to meet** her friends. And my parents **aren't going to be** there. They don't know it yet, but they**'re going to stay** in their room upstairs.

21 *Ellen:* **Are you going to cook spaghetti** for lunch?
Mum: **No, I'm not. I'm not going to cook** anything today.
Ellen: What **are we going to eat?**
Mum: You can have sandwiches. **I'm going to eat** in a restaurant.
Ellen: Oh, Mum. That's not fair.

22 1. He's going to visit his grandma in Manchester and he's going to go shopping.
2. No, he hasn't.
3. Because it was his birthday last week.
4. A Discman, new trainers or a mobile.
5. He must give Emily 20 pounds because she lent him 20 pounds last week.

23 A: Sarah tries some trousers on.
B: The waiter brought Sarah the wrong food.
C: Sarah can't find her size.
D: Sarah ordered a drink in a café.

24 A: Those trousers are nice, aren't they?
B: Yes, they are, but they're expensive.

A: You aren't going to buy those, are you?
B: Yes, I am.

152

A: You can't take all those in the changing rooms, can you?
B: Er, no. You're right.

A: Jean doesn't wear trainers, does she?
B: No, not usually.

25 Tom: **Excuse me.** Can you **bring us** the menu, **please?** And **we'd like** a glass of water and a cup of tea, please.
Waitress: Yes, of course. (…) Here are your drinks and here's the menu.
Tom: **Thanks.** The glass of water is **for me.** And can you **please tell me** what **today's special** is?
Waitress: Yes, it's chicken and chips.
Tom: OK. Then **I'd like** the special and my grandma **would like** the salad, **please.**

26 [e]: bread, lend, said, spend
[æ]: back, hang, have, salad

27 Dialogue A:
Girl: Excuse me. Can I try these trousers on, please?
Assistant: Yes, of course. The changing rooms are over there on the right.
Girl: Thanks.
Assistant: Do you like them?
Girl: Yes, I do, but they're too small. Have you got a larger size?
Assistant: Er. Let me look. Ah, yes, here we are.
Girl: Thanks. And where do I pay, please?
Assistant: Over there, near the door.
Girl: OK. Thank you.

1. In a clothes shop. – 2. Trousers. – 3. She wants to buy the trousers in a bigger size. – 4. Yes, she is.

Dialogue B:
Waiter: Hello. Can I help you?
Girl: Yes, what's today's special?
Waiter: It's spaghetti with fresh vegetables.
Girl: Er. I want the chicken and chips and a glass of water and my friend wants the cheese salad and a hot chocolate.
Waiter: OK. One chicken and chips and one cheese salad.
Girl: Hello. We need the bill now.
Waiter: OK. One minute please.
Girl: Wow, that's expensive. Is this bill right?

1. In a café. – 2. Spaghetti with fresh vegetables. – 3. Chicken and chips. – 4. No, she isn't.

Revision A (Unit 1–3)

1
school	→ subject	→ History/Art/P.E./Maths/Science
	→ school day	→ assembly/break/tutorial
in a café	→ on the table	→ fork/knife/plate/glass/spoon
	→ food	→ fruit/meat/vegetables/fish and chips

2 1. sandwiches; 2. chips; 3. burger; 4. fruit; 5. vegetables; 6. salad; 7. bacon and egg; 8. chocolate cake

3 1. to save; 2. change; 3. changing room; 4. supermarket

4
to lose ⟷ **to find**
to sell ⟷ **to buy**
to arrive ⟷ **to leave**
to get off ⟷ **to get on**
to cry ⟷ **to laugh**
to borrow ⟷ **to lend**
to save ⟷ **to spend**
to come ⟷ **to go**

5 What a day! I got up late and **left** the house. I ran to the station and **got on** the train – the wrong train. I changed trains and I **went** to town. I wanted to meet my friend Jane in a café at 12.30, but first I needed a birthday present. I went to my favourite shop and **bought** her a really nice present.
Then I bought a few presents for me, too. I **spent** all my money and then walked to the café. In the café Jane **lent** me some money for a drink and then I wanted to give Jane her birthday present but, where was my bag? I didn't have it. Jane looked at me and **laughed.** Then she said, "Are you looking for this? I **found** it in your favourite shop."

6 "What **are you going to do** next Saturday?" I asked my friends at school. "**I'm going to mend** my bike," said Ann. "And you**'re going to visit** your grandma, aren't you, Mike?" I wanted to meet them because it was my birthday on Saturday but I **didn't tell** them. It **was** my first year at school and so they didn't know it was my birthday. I **woke up** early on Saturday morning and I **got** some nice birthday presents from my mum and dad and my brother but I was sad. I wanted to meet my friends.
I **was watching** TV at about 4 o'clock when my mum said, "Can you walk

the dog, please, Chris?" It **was raining** and I **didn't want** to walk the dog, but I went. What a terrible birthday!
I **got back** at about 5 o'clock. While I **was walking** upstairs, my mum called, "**I'm washing** your clothes but there are some more on your bed." I went downstairs again and into the living room. It was full. All my friends and my family **were waiting** for me. It was a surprise party. "I **don't believe** it," I said. "This only **happens** in books."

7 At an underground station
You: **Hello. How much is a travelcard, please?**
Ticket office: It's three pounds eighty.
You: **And is there a special fare for children?**
Ticket office: Yes, it's one pound ninety.
You: **I'd like a travelcard for children then, please.**
Ticket office: Here you are.

In a café
You: **Excuse me. Can you bring us the menu, please?**
Waiter: Yes, of course.
You: **Thanks. And can you please tell me what today's special is?**
Waiter: It's spaghetti with fresh vegetables.
You: **I'd like two specials, please.**

8 Caroline: Did you have a good holiday?
Patrick: Yes, it was great. I love London. I'm sure it's the most exciting city in Britain.
Caroline: Yes, I love it there, too. What did you do?
Patrick: Well, we went on the London Eye, of course.
Caroline: Oh, the views from there are great, aren't they?
Patrick: Yes, they are, but they're not as good as the ones from Canary Wharf.
Caroline: Really?
Patrick: Yes, my uncle works there so we went there, too. And we went shopping and we spent lots of time in Covent Garden.
Caroline: Oh, Covent Garden's great, isn't it?
Patrick: Yes, I think it's the most interesting place in London. You can always watch something there or somebody. Oh, and something funny happened there, too.
Caroline: What?
Patrick: Well, I was sitting there in a café when I heard somebody say hello. I turned around and saw Emma.
Caroline: No! What was she doing in London?
Patrick: She was visiting her sister and guess what!
Caroline: What!

Patrick: Her sister lives two streets away from my uncle.
Caroline: No! Isn't London small?
Patrick: Yes. A village.

1. right; 2. wrong; 3. wrong; 4. wrong; 5. right; 6. wrong

9 The pupils are at school. They're sitting in a classroom and they're listening to a teacher. One boy isn't listening. He's thinking about the weekend. At the weekend he's going to meet some friends and they're going to play football. A girl is thinking about the weekend, too. She's going to go to London. She's going to go shopping and she's going to go on the London Eye.

Unit 4

1 1. singing lessons; 2. fashion model; 3. game show; 4. singles charts; 5. film star; 6. boy band

2 Last year I joined a band.
I must give a presentation about the band at school.
We're going to go for a picnic after we've practiced next time.
We're going to do the shopping for the picnic after school.
Most singers don't make much money.
It's more important to have fun.
I'm going to take photos.

3 I want to be a **film star,**
And have a racing car.
I want to be an **actor**
and go to parties after
every film I make
is that a big **mistake?**
I want to be a dancer
or maybe a football **player**

who scores with every **shot**
and goes to parties a lot.
I'd like to be a **drummer**
or maybe a famous singer
at the top of the **charts**
breaking fans' hearts
but I'm not a great **success**
at singing and all the rest.
But at one thing I'm the best,
I'm the greatest **speller!** Yes!

4

T	E	A	S	E	J	P	U	S	H
R	D	U	I	X	A	K	E	C	K
A	Q	D	V	D	Y	E	T	O	Q
I	Y	I	E	N	D	F	Z	R	D
N	N	T	R	F	G	K	U	E	S
M	G	I	V	E	U	P	A	S	J
P	T	O	B	E	L	B	L	S	H
U	Z	N	A	L	O	J	O	I	N

tease; push; train; audition, give up; feel; dye; score, join

5 If you want a part in a play, you must usually **audition.**
Football players usually **train** for a few hours every day.
I **joined** an orchestra when I was ten.
I **felt** really nervous when I first auditioned.
I **scored** my first goal yesterday. It was great.
My parents have never **pushed** me but they've always helped me.
My friends often **tease** me now that they can see me on TV.
It was difficult at first but I never **gave up.**
I **dyed** my hair when I joined the band.

6 Have you ever **met** a film star? – No, but I've **been** in a film.
Have you ever **sung** a song on stage? – No, but I've **written** a song which was in the charts.
Have you ever **found** lots of money? – No, but I've **lost** lots of money.
Have you ever **bought** a car? – No, but I've **sold** a bike.
Have you ever **seen** a famous actor on stage? – No, but I've **heard** a famous singer in the park.

4 | **Lösungen**

7 Have you **ever** met somebody famous? – No, I've **never** met anybody famous.
Have you made a CD **yet?** – Yes, we've made two **so far.**

8 Paul: **Did you watch** that singing competition on TV last night?
Mike: No, **I didn't. Was it** good?
Paul: No, **it wasn't.** The singers **were** terrible. Nobody's going to become a star. So what **did you do?**
Mike: I **went** to the theatre.
Paul: You **didn't watch** a play, **did you?**
Mike: No, **I didn't.** I **auditioned** for a part in a play.
Paul: **Did you get** it?
Mike: Yes, **I did.**
Paul: Wow. So you're going to become a star.

9 John hasn't acted on stage.
He has practised really hard for the play.
I have just watched the play.
I haven't seen a better actor .

10 John has just arrived at the theatre. He has felt nervous all day.

11
kaufen	to buy	bought	bought
fallen	to fall	fell	fallen
hören	to hear	heard	heard
lesen	to read	read	read
sehen	to see	saw	seen

12 Jane has **heard** a great song on the radio and so she's just **bought** a new CD. Jane's at home now and she's just **seen** a picture of the singer, and she's **fallen** in love with him. He's very good-looking. It's evening now and Jane's in the living room. She's just **read** an interview with the singer in a magazine. "What a silly man!" she thinks. She's not in love with him now.

13 A: Have you ever sung a song on stage?
B: No, I haven't, but I've sung lots of songs in the bathroom.
A: How has Phil practised for the competition?
B: His friends have helped him.
A: Has Tina ever acted in a play on TV?
B: She has not been on TV yet.

14 Ann: United's manager **has asked** you to play in their first team. How do you feel?
Steve: It's a dream. I**'ve been** a United fan all my life.
Ann: You've got an important match on Saturday. **Have you played** with United before?
Steve: No, **I haven't,** but **I've trained** with them, of course.
Ann: You **haven't finished** school yet. How **have you practised** with United?
Steve: I**'ve practised** with them every morning and I**'ve had** special lessons in the afternoon or evening.
Ann: **Has the manager given** you some tips for the game?
Steve: No, **he hasn't.** I **haven't spoken** to him yet but the team's going to meet tomorrow morning.

15 Have you ever met a famous person? – Yes, I have. I've talked to a famous actor a few times. He's never answered me.

16 Have you ever fallen in love?
Have you bought a poster of your favourite pop star yet?
I've already written two letters to him.

17 A: Have you **ever** sung in a band?
B: No, I've **never** sung in a band but I've **already** sung on stage four times.
A: Have you made any singles **yet?**
B: Yes, I've made two **so far** but nobody has bought them **yet.** And I've **just/already** written two new songs.

18 1.
A: What did you do yesterday?
B: I practised with the band.
→ **yesterday/simple past**
2.
A: Have you seen his new film yet?
B: No, I haven't.
→ **yet/present perfect**
3.
A: Has the party already started?
B: No, it hasn't.
→ **already/present perfect**

4.
A: When did John go to Hollywood?
B: He went about two years ago, but he doesn't like it.
→ **(two years) ago/simple past**
5.
A: I've never been to the cinema.
B: No. You're joking.
→ **never/present perfect**
6.
A: When did he make that CD?
B: In 2004.
→ **in (2004)/simple past**

19 Rob: **Have you ever been** on TV, Liz?
Liz: Yes, **I've been** in two game shows so far.
Rob: Really? When **were you** in a game show then?
Liz: Well, last week I **was** in a spelling competition.
Rob: **Did you win** anything?
Liz: Yes, I **won** some money, but **I've already spent** it.

20 How many competitions have you already won?
I've won two so far.
Great. And have you ever danced with a famous dancer?
Yes, I have. Last week I danced with a world champion.
And was it better than before?
Yes, it was much easier. And it was great fun.

21 Anna's e-mails: first – **C**; second – **F**; third – **E**
Jim's e-mails: first – **A**; second – **D**; third – **B**

22 1. right; 2. wrong; 3. right; 4. right; 5. wrong; 6. right; 7. wrong

23 1.
A: Are you hungry?
B: No, thanks. I've had lunch.
→ **a**
2.
A: She's won the match. Yeah, it's great.
→ **a**
3.
A: What did you get in town on Saturday?
B: We bought some new CDs.
→ **b**

24 Our presentation is about Alfred Hitchcock. First, we'd like to say a few words about his life and then about his films. We're going to show a few interesting parts from his films and finally we're going to explain why his films were so important. If you have any questions, we can answer them after our presentation.
Alfred Hitchcock was born in London in 1899 and stayed there until he was 40. After that he lived in California until he died in 1980. He made his first film in the UK in 1922 and he made over 50 films in his life. Here's a list of all the films he made. (…) Have you got any questions? No? OK. Well, we hope you enjoyed our presentation and thanks for your attention.

7 – We hope you enjoyed our presentation.
2 – First, we'd like to say a few words about … and then …
6 – Have you got any questions?
X – Let's work together.
4 – If you have any questions, we can answer them after our presentation.
5 – Here's a list of …
3 – And finally we're going to …
1 – Our presentation is about …
X – Who's going to talk about …?

25 1.
Hi. I'm sitting in the park. (…) No, I haven't played football today, they didn't need me. Are you at home? (…) What? You're doing your homework on a Saturday? (…) No. Guess what! I've just heard from the drama school. (…) Yes, they sent me a letter. I can start in September. (…) Yeah. I'm really happy. (…) Great. See you this evening then.
2.
Hi. No, I didn't get the part. (…) Yeah. I heard from the theatre yesterday. (…) Yes, I didn't feel very good yesterday but I've forgotten all that now. (…) No, no. I spent last evening with Lisa and I've fallen in love. (…) Yes. You heard me. Yeah, she kissed me this morning.
3.
Hi Emma? (…) Yeah, I'm in the park. And how are you? (…) What? You've just heard from the theatre? (…) You've got the part? (…) Great! (…) Yeah, I've just played football with some friends and I'm going home now. (…) You're having a party this evening? (…) Great. See you later then.

1. **C;** 2. **D;** 3. **A**

26

1.
No, he hasn't.
He's going to start drama school.
2.
He feels great because he's fallen in love.
3.
He's going to go to a party because his friend, Emma, has got a part in a play.

Unit 5

1

R	P	W	A	N	W	E	T	R	P	I	W	E
O	R	I	E	N	T	E	E	R	I	N	G	R
E	K	Q	R	A	U	O	W	E	L	D	F	T
J	U	D	O	D	S	U	R	F	I	N	G	E
O	L	D	B	L	D	K	J	L	M	B	A	Q
I	N	L	I	N	E	S	K	A	T	I	N	G
G	R	O	C	K	C	L	I	M	B	I	N	G
U	C	V	S	F	D	J	H	W	A	E	T	K

orienteering; rock climbing; aerobics; judo; in-line skating; surfing

2
When you **go orienteering,** you must run and read a map.
When you **go rock climbing,** you usually go to the hills but you can also use a wall in a sports centre.
I **do aerobics** because I want to keep fit.
I **do judo** because it's fun and you must be quick. It's not about fights.
I **do/go in-line skating** in a park. It's dangerous on the road.
I always **go surfing** in the sea on holiday.

3 1. compass; 2. anorak; 3 equipment; 4. canoe; 5. life-jacket

4 Kopfschmerz – he**a**dache; Rezept – presc**ri**ption; Schmerz – p**ai**n; Tablette – ta**b**let; Gesundheit – h**e**alth; Krankenhaus – hospi**t**al; Unfall – accid**e**nt; Fitness – fitne**s**s
Lösungswort: diabetes

5 1. swimmer; 2. reader; 3. reporter; 4. trainer; 5. bully; 6. doctor

6 1. head, eye, ear
   nose, mouth, neck
2. back, arm, leg, foot, toe,
   shoulder, stomach, hand, finger, knee

7 gesund – **healthy**
verärgert – **angry**
übergewichtig – **overweight**
schnell – **quick**
schwer – **heavy**
krank – **sick**
nass – **wet**

8 Every morning I **jog** for an hour because I want to **keep fit.** I like food and I eat a lot but I don't **weigh** too much because I run so often. It's great.
I usually feel really good in the morning but one morning I was **jogging** and I **bumped into** a tree, fell and then **hit** my head on something. It **bled** so much that I had to go to hospital. The doctor **examined** me and asked, "So what were you doing?" I told him and he said, "Yes, sport isn't always healthy, is it?"

9 1. object; 2. object; 3. subject; 4. object; 5. subject; 6. subject; 7. object; 8. subject

10 What do you do in the evening?
TV or sport. Which do you like best?
Who helps you when you have a problem?
What makes you happy?
Who do you look after?

11 – **Who cooks** at home usually?
+ I usually cook.
– **What do you like** to cook most?
+ like to cook vegetables and fish.
– **Which are** healthier – chips or salads?

+ They are both fine, but you mustn't eat too much of anything.
- **Who would you like** to cook for?
+ I'd like to cook for children who have only ever eaten fish and chips.

12
1. Where were you riding to?
2. What was your horse looking at?
3. What were you thinking about?
4. When your horse suddenly stopped, what did you fall into?
5. What was the party like?

13
Jean laughs happily.
Robert talks quietly.
She sings beautifully.
He acts terribly.
She reads well.
He runs fast.

14
I'm a **good** tennis player but Mathew plays **well,** too, and he almost always wins. Last Saturday I really wanted to win. I was **fit** and I was playing **brilliantly.** The game started **well.** Mathew hit the ball **hard** but I was **quick** and I almost always got it back again.
After two hours I only needed one more game to win, but I was getting **tired** and Mathew was still playing **beautifully.** He won the next game **easily** and my feet were hurting **terribly.**
"Oh no, I'm going to lose again," I thought, but then I was very **lucky** – it started raining and we stopped for 20 minutes. That was enough and I won the match. I've never been so **happy** about rain before, but next time we play, I'm going to be fitter.

15
1.
Are you lucky? – Yes, I am. I often win things.
⟶ **lucky – Adjektiv**
2.
Do you know him? – Yes, he's in my class. He always works hard.
⟶ **hard – Adverb**
3.
Do you like her? – Yes, she's very friendly.
⟶ **friendly – Adjektiv**
4.
What do you usually eat? – Fruit, vegetables. I always eat healthily.
⟶ **healthily – Adverb**

16 Daniel runs **fast,** but Mary runs **faster** and Chris runs **fastest.**
Chris eats **healthily,** but Daniel eats **more healthily** and Mary eats **most healthily.**
Mary plays football **well,** Daniel plays football **better** and Chris plays football **best.**
Chris climbs **safely,** but Daniel climbs **more safely** and Chris climbs **most safely.**

17 On Wednesday the 10th of September I left school late. I was walking home at about 16.30 when I saw John Evans in front of me. He was walking past the park when three boys came out of the park. They walked behind him for a few minutes and then they walked next to him. Suddenly he shouted, "Give me my Discman back." They hit him and he fell on the floor. They kicked him and I shouted at them. I ran to help John but the three boys ran away. I called the police on my mobile and after about ten minutes the police arrived.

18 1. wrong; 2. wrong; 3. right; 4. wrong; 5. right; 6. wrong

19 I've hurt my shoulder. → **D**
My stomach hurts. → **B**
I've broken my leg. → **A**
I've got a headache. → **C**
I feel sick. → **E**
I've just been sick. → **E**
I've got a temperature. → **C**
I haven't eaten anything today. → **B** oder **E**

Dialog 1: C
Doctor: Hello, Jane. Come in and sit down.
Jane: Hello.
Doctor: How can I help you today?
Jane: Oh, I feel terrible. I think I've got a temperature and I've got a headache. And my arms hurt and my legs hurt and I just want to sleep all day.
Doctor: OK. Well, let me just examine you. Does this hurt?
Jane: Ow.
Doctor: Yes, well. I think you've got the flu. And there's nothing I can give you for that so you must just go home and stay in bed for a few days until you feel better.

Dialog 2: A
Doctor: Hello, Peter. What have you done?
Peter: I've broken my leg.
Doctor: How did you do that?

5 Lösungen

Peter: I fell off my bike when I was in France last week. And the doctor at the hospital told me to come and see you when I got home again.
Doctor: How does it feel? Does it still hurt?
Peter: No, not really.
Doctor: Well, there's nothing I can do for you now. Wait two more weeks and then go to hospital. They can check it there for you again.
Peter: OK. Thank you.

Dialog 3: E
Ann: Hello, Dr Jenkins. I feel sick. Can you help me?
Doctor: Have you eaten anything which was bad?
Ann: No, I don't think so. I haven't eaten anything today.
Doctor: Have you been sick?
Ann: Yes, I've just been sick and I was sick this morning, too.
Doctor: Well, let me just examine your stomach. Does this hurt?
Ann: No.
Doctor: OK. I think you've got stomach flu and there's nothing I can give you for that. Don't eat anything today or tomorrow but drink a lot of tea with sugar in and water.

Dialog 4: B
Doctor: Hello, James. How are you feeling today?
James: Well, my stomach still hurts, Doctor, and I can't eat much.
Doctor: Have the tablets helped?
James: No, not really.
Doctor: Well, I can give you some other tablets. Here's a prescription. Take two tablets every evening.

Dialog 5: D
Steve: Hello, Doctor. I've hurt my shoulder. Can you help me or do I need to go to hospital?
Doctor: Well, let me look at it. Can you move your fingers?
Steve: Yes, but it hurts.
Doctor: Mm. And can you move your arm?
Steve: Ow.
Doctor: OK. Well, I don't think anything's broken so you don't need to go to hospital. Look! Here's a prescription. Take two tablets four times a day for the pain.

20
1. She must go home and stay in bed for a few days.
2. He must go to the hospital in two weeks.
3. She mustn't eat anything today or tomorrow and she must drink a lot of tea with sugar in and water.
4. He must take two tablets every evening.
5. He must take two tablets four times a day for the pain.

21
1. park; 2. right; 3. bag; 4. had; 5. pig; 6. do; 7. heart; 8. could; 9. pack; 10. but; 11. goal; 12. class

22

Interviewer:	Hello Liz. It's great to have you here.
Liz:	Thanks Paul.
Interviewer:	Now you've just won a big orienteering competition. How do you feel?
Liz:	Great. I trained really hard for the competition and I was very fit so I thought I could win, but you always need to be lucky, too. And I was.
Interviewer:	So tell me about your day. How do you keep fit and train for competitions?
Liz:	Well, I go orienteering every weekend with my club and I run every day, too. I usually run about a mile in the morning before breakfast. In the evening I do different sports. On Mondays and Wednesdays I do aerobics and Tuesdays and Thursdays I go swimming.
Interviewer:	And Fridays?
Liz:	Oh, on Fridays I always go out with my friends. I need a break, too.
Interviewer:	And what about food? Must you be careful about what you eat?
Liz:	Yes, and no. I love food and I can eat everything that I like really. But I mustn't eat too many sweet things or too many chips and burgers, of course.
Interviewer:	So you're fit and that's very important for orienteering. But you can also read maps well. How did you learn that?
Liz:	Well, I've always loved maps. I always read the maps for my mum or dad in the car when we go on holiday.
Interviewer:	And you always get to the right place?
Liz:	Yes, of course. Oh, but we did have problems once.
Interviewer:	Oh, what happened?

Liz: Well, we were in France on holiday and we were going home. We were driving at night because we wanted to take the first boat in the morning. And anyway we found the right road, the A6, I think, and I knew that we needed to stay on that road for about an hour so I just closed my eyes. When I opened them again, I saw that we were near the south of France. We were on the right road but we were driving south and not north. That's because I didn't have my compass with me.

1. Orienteering.
2. She goes every weekend.
3. On Mondays and Wednesdays.
4. She meets her friends.
5. No, there isn't.
6. When they go on holiday.
7. Because they wanted to go home to England and they were going south and not north.

Revision B (Unit 4–5)

1 A **doctor** often writes a **prescription**.
A **football player** always wants to win the **match**.
A **singer** wants to be at the top of the **charts**.
An **actor** wants **success**.
A **fashion model** must sometimes wear a **suit**.

2 parts of your body: knee, neck, stomach, toe
health: headache, pain, sick, temperature
sport: aerobics, judo, orienteering, rock climbing

3 aufgeben – to give up; auslachen – to laugh at; zusammenstoßen – to bump into; wählen – to vote for; anlächeln – to smile at

4
1. When you know what a word means, you **understand** it.
2. When something red comes out of your knee, for example, you **bleed**.
3. When a doctor looks at somebody, he or she **examines** her or him.
4. When something goes from one place to another, it **moves**.
5. If you are not careful, you **risk** an accident.
6. If you tell somebody something that they have forgotten, you **remind** them.
7. When you colour your hair, you **dye** it.
8. I **weigh** more than you but I'm not overweight.
9. When you want a part in a play, you must **audition**.

Lösungswort: When you explain yourself, you **give reasons**.

5
Have you every played a trick on your English teacher?
What did you do yesterday?
I've never climbed a mountain.

6
I**'ve never been** on stage but I've always wanted to act in a play. My problem is that I**'ve always been** nervous. A few weeks ago I **saw** a poster. It said that they were looking for young actors for a play. I wanted to go but I **didn't think** that I could. I **knew** that people from my school wanted to audition and I'm always more nervous when I know people. Then I had a brilliant idea. I **dyed** my hair and wore sunglasses. It worked. I **felt** really cool with the sunglasses and I auditioned really well. Then as I **was leaving** the theatre, John, a boy from my school shouted, "Cool sunglasses, Nick!" How embarrassing! But it wasn't a problem. I**'ve already heard** from the theatre and yes! I've got the part.

7
Cinema News: Hello Sasha. It's great to have you here.
Sasha Darnell: Thank you. It's nice to be here.
Cinema News: I'd like to ask you about your life. How did you become an actor?
Sasha Darnell: Well, it started at school. I wasn't very good at school but when I did funny things, people laughed. I liked that so I acted in school plays.
Cinema News: Who helped you at school?
Sasha Darnell: Ted Smith. He's a good English teacher and he can explain very well.
Cinema News: And who have you learnt most from?
Sasha Darnell: I've learnt most from my mum. She always laughs even when things don't go well.

B | **Lösungen**

8 Emily and Helen are both very good at sport. They play tennis and go in-line skating. They had tennis lessons when they were very small. They both run fast but Helen runs faster maybe because she is taller. Helen won the 100 metres race in the Bristol School's competition in 2008. They also both dance but Emily dances more beautifully than Helen. Emily has won many dance competitions and she wants to become a dancer. Helen wants to become a doctor. They do some sport every evening but they don't do aerobics or jog.

Interviewer: Hello Helen. Hello Emily. It's great to have you here.
Emily: Thank you. It's nice to be here.
Helen: Thank you.
Interviewer: Now. You are both very good at sport and dancing. How did that happen, Helen?
Helen: Well, our parents both like sport, so we've always done sport, too. We had tennis lessons when we were very small.
Interviewer: And you both run fast.
Emily: Yes, Helen runs faster but she's taller than me, too.
Interviewer: But you have won competitions, too, Emily.
Emily: Well, I haven't really won any, but I often come second. Helen always wins. She won the Bristol Schools' Competition in 2008.
Interviewer: Yes, congratulations, Helen. Did you train hard for that?
Helen: Yes, I did, but I always train hard because I enjoy it.
Interviewer: But how do you find the time?
Helen: Well, we usually do our homework at school and then we've got time in the evening. We usually do some sport every evening and it's fun. We see our friends there and we keep fit, too. We needn't do aerobics or jog or anything like that.
Interviewer: Oh, I see, so one sport helps the other.
Helen: Yes, well, all sports are different but they're all easier when you're fit.
Interviewer: So that helps your dancing, too? Because you both dance well, too, don't you?
Helen: Yes, well, Emily dances more beautifully. She's a great dancer and she's won lots of competitions.
Interviewer: Would you like to become a dancer, Emily?
Emily: Yes, I would.
Interviewer: And you, Helen?
Helen: I want to become a doctor.

Unit 6

1 The guitar and the drums are **musical instruments.**
The **bagpipes** are an old Scottish instrument.
At a **ceilidh** you dance to old Scottish music.
Lots of people **hike** in the Scottish mountains.
Many people go **fishing** in the Scottish lochs or rivers.

2 **Work** in Scotland has changed a lot in the last fifty years. A lot or maybe most people worked in fishing or on farms and in small factories in the past. Now the **oil industry** has changed Scotland a lot. Many people work on **oil platforms** or have other jobs where they work with oil. Oil has made some towns in Scotland rich but it is not only oil which has changed life for **workers** in Scotland. There are now also many **high-tech** jobs in **offices** there.

3 It's going to **rain** tomorrow.
It's often **windy** near the coast.
There are often **clouds** over the hills.
It can be dangerous on an oil platform when there's a **thunderstorm.**
We're going to have a beautiful **sunny** day tomorrow.
It's difficult to land a helicopter when there's lots of **fog.**

4 I'm not a **soldier** but I'm a Scot and I'm fighting so that I can be free. The English steal my land and **kill** my sons; I must fight them. I am not a **hero** but I have known a few – men who have risked or given their lives for other people although they were scared.
I have **fought** many **battles** but I'm getting old now and maybe this was my last. I have been caught by my **enemy.** Will they kill me or just keep me **prisoner?** I don't know but I hope hope the future will be better for the Scots.

5 down: 1. pati**e**nt; 2. **g**entle; 3. k**i**nd; 6. weak
across: 2. **g**lad; 4. th**i**n; 5. hot-head**e**d; 7. per**f**ect
Lösungswort: interesting

6 schicken – to send; besitzen – to own; versprechen – to promise; hoffen – to hope; teilen – to share

7 1. excited; 2. angry; 3. nervous; 4. sad; 5. glad

8 Excuse me, please. Where can I buy stamps? – At that shop over there.
Is there a post office near here? – Yes, it's opposite the station.
How much is a postcard to Germany? – It's 35 p.
Where is the nearest postbox, please? – It's in front of the newsagent.
I'd like five stamps for Germany, please. – Here you are.

9
Sue: Look! Here's the waiter with our dinner.
John: No, that's not **ours.** Look! It's **theirs.** He's going to their table.
Sue: Oh yes. But here is **ours.** Look, that's our waiter.
John: Thank you. The fish. That's **mine.** Yes, I ordered that. And the chicken – that's **yours,** isn't it, Sue?
Sue: No, it's not **mine.** I ordered chicken with fresh vegetables.
Waiter: Oh, I'm sorry. I think, it's **his** over there. He hasn't got his meal yet.

10 1.
Girl: Oh, look! Pete has forgotten his anorak.
Boy: But that's not Pete's. It's mine.
⟶ 1. **mine – Pronomen**
2.
Girl 1: Oh no. I've lost my mobile.
Girl 2: No, you haven't. I saw it in the house this morning.
⟶ 2. **my – Begleiter**
3.
Girl 1: Hey. Whose is that camera? Is it Ben's?
Girl 2: No, it isn't his. He hasn't got his with him.
⟶ 3. **his – Pronomen**
4.
Girl: We must remember our sandwiches.
Boy: Yes, they're in the kitchen.
⟶ 4. **our – Begleiter**
5.
Girl: Have you got your compass?
Boy: No, I haven't, but we don't need one today, do we?
⟶ 5. **your – Begleiter**
6.
Girl 1: Hey, Jean. What are you doing? Those shoes aren't yours?
Girl 2: Ah. That's why I can't get my feet into them.
⟶ 6. **yours – Pronomen**

11 The weather will be nice.
I'm sure we'll meet some nice people there.
John thinks he'll go to a Ceilidh.
My cousins promise they'll show us the mountains.
I hope we'll hear some bagpipes.
I'm sure you'll have a good time.

12
1. Will I need an anorak? – Yes, you will. It will rain tomorrow.
2. Will we see the Loch Ness Monster? – No, we won't. It won't want to talk to us.
3. Will we catch some fish? – Yes, we will. I'm sure we'll be lucky.
4. Will you swim in the loch? – No, I won't. It won't be warm enough.
5. Will Aunt Jane visit us? – No, she won't. She won't be in Scotland next week.

13 I think you'll leave Scotland. – No, I won't. I'll never leave Scotland.
Will John become a footballer? – No, he won't. He won't train hard enough.
Will we be friends in ten years? – No, we won't. I'll be rich and famous and won't want to know you.

14
1. **We** play against Edinburgh on Saturday.
2. **We'll** play well.
3. You **don't** like football.
4. You **won't** enjoy the match.
5. **We'll** win, I know.

15
1. *Going-to*-Futur: Man kann voraussehen, was passieren wird.
2. *Will*-Futur: Es handelt sich um eine Vermutung.
3. *Going-to*-Futur: Es handelt sich um einen Plan.
4. *Will*-Futur: Es handelt sich nicht um einen Plan.

16 What time are you going to get there?
I'm not sure. I think we'll leave home about 6 o'clock.
Will there be lots of people there?
Yes, all my friends are going to go.

17
Ben: What **are you going to do** on Saturday?
Kate: I**'m going to go** to Roger's birthday party. **Are you going to go,** too?
Ben: No, **I'm not.** He hasn't invited me – I forgot to invite him to my party.
Kate: I'm sure you**'ll get** one. He**'ll be** 16 and he**'s going to have** a really big party.
Ben: **Is he going to have** a ceilidh?

Kate: No, **he isn't.** He**'s going to have** a disco and I think they**'ll have** some games there, too.
Ben: Oh, that sounds good. I hope he **won't forget** me.

18 If we take the first train, we'll get there at 10 o'clock.
The shops won't be open if we get there so early.
If you have time, you must visit the castle there.
If you like, I'll give you my cousin's phone number.
If she has time, she'll show you around.
Take some good shoes with you if you want to see a lot.
You'll see more interesting things if a Scot shows you around.
It won't be a problem if you don't have much money.
If you go to the right places, you'll hear some great music.

19 1. If I **go** to the Ceilidh, I**'ll see** Kate. I**'ll be** very happy if I **see** Kate. I **won't be** happy if she**'s** with another boy.
2. Well, she **won't dance** with me if I **don't ask** her. If I **dance** with her, it**'ll be** embarrassing – I can't dance. Maybe if I just **talk** to her, she **won't want** to dance.
3. If I **have** dancing lessons, I**'ll learn** to dance well. If I **ask** her, maybe Kate **will teach** me. If she **teaches** me to dance, maybe she**'ll want** to go to Ceilidhs every week. Hm! Maybe I**'ll find** a girl who likes football if I**'m** lucky.

20 If you go to the Highlands, you will see lots of wild animals.
You must take warm clothes if you want to climb the mountains.
Be very careful if it is foggy.
If you climb Ben Nevis, you will have a great view.

21 *Maggie:* Oh, did I tell you? We're going to go to Scotland next week on holiday.
William: Oh great. **When** you get there, will you send me a postcard?
Maggie: I'll send you one **if** I can find a postbox. We're going to stay in the Highlands for the first week. Then we're going to stay with my aunt in Inverness and maybe my cousins will be there. **If** they are there, they'll take us to parties.
William: Oh, that's nice. **When** you're there, will you visit Loch Ness?
Maggie: I'm not sure. **If** we've got time, I think we'll go there.
William: Well, **if** you go there, you must look for the Loch Ness Monster. And **if** you see it, you must go to the doctor's right away.
Maggie: Hah hah. Very funny.

22 1. *Alan:* excited, positive (line 17), happy (line 22)
Brian: happy (line 22), calm (line 46)
Simon: bored (line 3), happy (line 22), scared (line 38)
2. Alan: Yeah, I think we'll be OK (line 12) / Oh, we won't go that near (line 28) / That's near enough (line 32) → These show that Alan is more careful.
Simon: No, that's boring (line 3) / Brian, you're not scared of a bit of water, are you? (line 7) / Oh, we'll have our compasses (line 10) / Brian, you're not scared …? (line 7) → These show that Simon is a bit silly. He doesn't think about things.
Simon: I can't go (line 43) → This shows Simon was scared and could not act when he needed, too.
Brian: Are you both crazy? (line 26) → This shows that Brian was careful and didn't want to take risks.
Brian: (line 41) We must go for help. → This shows that Brian was very brave (mutig).
3. Alan feels excited when he comes out of the cloud and sees the sun and the eagle and that's why he goes to the nest.
Simon feels excited, too, and he is very silly and that is why he goes too near the eagle's nest. After the accident he feels scared and nervous and he can't go and get help.
Brian is very careful and maybe a bit nervous at the beginning of the story. He's also scared after the accident but he stays cool and goes and gets help.

23 I can **see the sea** from my bedroom.
I'm going to go to town **by bus and I think I'll buy** a new skirt.
Where will you wear the skirt?
I think I'll dye my hair red tomorrow.
Their sandwiches are **over there.**

24 *Regen- und Windsymbole an der Westküste, vor allem bei Glasgow.*
Gewitter, Regen- und Windsymbole in den Highlands.
Sonnensymbole an der Ostküste von Edinburgh bis Aberdeen.
Wolkensymbole bei Inverness.
Nebelsymbole bei den Inseln im Norden und Westen.

Weatherman:	At the moment we have beautiful sunny weather all over Scotland, but this summer weather is going to change over the weekend and on Saturday we're going to have some rain in the west of Scotland.
Radio presenter:	Does that mean it'll rain on the England-Scotland football match?

Weatherman: Yes, I'm sure it'll rain in Glasgow on Saturday and it will also be very windy.
Radio presenter: Yuk. Well, I think I'll watch the game in my living room.
Weatherman: In the Highlands the weather will be even worse. We're going to have thunderstorms with heavy rain and strong winds.
Radio presenter: So anybody who wanted to hike in the Highlands at the weekend, should think again?
Weatherman: Yes, if you want to hike, you'll be better on the east coast. There the weather will be still very sunny and warm on Saturday – well, from about Edinburgh to Aberdeen. Farther north, around Inverness, it'll be cloudy although it shouldn't rain there. The rain will come to the east coast and the far north on Sunday.
Radio presenter: What about the Orkneys and the Hebrides?
Weatherman: Well, it won't rain there but the weather won't be very nice either. It'll be cold and foggy.
Radio presenter: And on Sunday?
Weatherman: It'll be rainy all over Scotland but we won't have the strong winds.
Radio presenter: So the weather won't be nice at the weekend but we've got lots of things for you inside. There's a ceilidh on Saturday night …

25 Dear Pete,
We're having a **great time here in Scotland.** Every day we **hike** in **the mountains** and the weather is **great.** It's **sunny** and warm every day and we even **go swimming** in the rivers. Yes, they're very cold but it's **great fun.** Tomorrow we're **going to climb** Ben Nevis. That will be **hard,** I think. In the picture you can see **Loch Ness.** We **visited** there on our first day here and no, we didn't see the monster. Have a good holiday.
CU
Nic

Nic: Hi. It's me.
Mum: Nic. How are you? Are you having a good time?
Nic: Yes, it's great. Even the weather's great.
Mum: You mean, it's not raining.
Nic: No, it's been sunny and warm every day.
Mum: Well, you're lucky. It's raining here in Manchester. What are you doing there?
Nic: Well, we hike in the mountains every day. And you know what? It's so warm, we even go swimming in the rivers.
Mum: Aren't they cold?

Nic: Yes, but it's great fun.
Mum: Have you visited Loch Ness yet?
Nic: Yes, we went there on the first day.
Mum: Did you see the Loch Ness Monster?
Nic: No, Mum.
Mum: What are you going to do tomorrow?
Nic: We're going to climb Ben Nevis.
Mum: Oh, wow. Are you so fit?
Nic: Oh, Mum. You know I'm fit, but yes, I think it will be hard.
Mum: Well, don't climb too quickly and remember your …
Nic: Oh, Mum. I must go now. Somebody's calling me for dinner.
Mum: OK Nic. Well, have a good time.

26
Jean: Did you have a good time yesterday evening at the Ceilidh?
Sarah: Yes, Jean, it was great. It was really good fun. We danced all night.
Tim: Yes, even I enjoyed it and I'm terrible at dancing.
Jean: That's good. I'm glad you enjoyed it. And where are you going today?
Tim: Oh, we're going to hike in the mountains somewhere.
Jean: That'll be nice. Would you like to take some sandwiches with you?
Sarah: Yes, please, Jean. That's a good idea.
Jean: And have you got anoraks and pullovers with you?
Tim: No, but it's a beautiful day. Look! It's really sunny.
Jean: Yes, but the weather can change very quickly and although it's warm down here, it won't be as warm up in the mountains.
Sarah: I'm glad you told us – I'll just go and get some pullovers and anoraks.
Jean: And don't forget the long trousers.
Jean: OK. Here are your sandwiches and something to drink. And have you got a compass?
Tim: A compass? We're just going to walk on good paths where there are signs.
Jean: Yes, but if it gets foggy, you won't see the signs.
Tim: Oh no. Look! I can't get everything into my bag now. I've got too many things to carry.
Sarah: I know. Let's just go to the coast and then we won't have too much to carry.
Tim: Good idea.

1. They went to a ceilidh and danced all night. Yes, they both enjoyed it.
2. Pullovers, anoraks, long trousers, sandwiches, something to drink and a compass because the weather can change quickly and it's often cold at the top of mountains.

Unit 7

1
1. You can fly in a **plane.**
2. When you arrive at the airport, you go to the **check-in.**
3. If you want to travel over the sea, you can go by **ferry.**
4. When you travel from one country to another, you often need to take your **passport** with you.
5. You collect your bags in a **hall.**
6. Your plane maybe late so you must listen for an **announcement.**
7. A **shuttle** is a special train that goes between two places.
8. **Baggage** is another name for all your bags.
9. If you're meeting somebody who has just landed at the airport, go to **arrivals.**
10. Go to **departures** if you want to fly somewhere.
11. If the weather is very bad, your **flight** may be late.
12. When you've got your baggage, you must go through **customs.**
13. At some airports there is more than one **terminal.**

2 Lerner – learner; Kurs – course; Unterricht – lesson; Grammatik – grammar; Gastfamilie – host family; Freunde finden – to make friends

3 **May I have** a glass of water? – Yes, of course. I'll get you one.
Shall I help you with the dinner? – Oh, yes, please. That would be nice.
Could you lend me a map, please? – Yes, there's one on the bookshelf.
What shall I do with my dirty jeans? – Oh, give them to me. I'll wash them tomorrow.
Is it OK if I phone my parents? – Yes, of course. You can take the phone into your bedroom.

4 alien – außerirdisch; earth – Erde; earthquake – Erdbeben; sky – Himmel; planet – Planet

5 Last year I wanted to **improve** my Spanish and so I went to Spain for a month and did a language course. It was great fun but I had a few problems, too. My first problem was that I hate flying so while we were **taking off** my legs **were shaking** more than the plane. The second problem was that I **missed** my friends at first, but then I **made friends** with lots of the people on the course and didn't miss my friends at home at all. The third problem was that I couldn't understand anybody because everybody spoke so fast. I **got used to** that though – after about three and a half weeks! It was my best holiday ever and now I'm home again I can't **imagine** that I almost didn't go because I was scared!

6 May I have a glass of water, please? – Shall I put my bags in my room? – Could you tell me where the language school is? – Could I look at the garden, please?

7 *Teacher:* **Could** you all wait over there, please?
Student: **May/Could** I look at your book, please? I've forgotten mine.

Student 1: **Shall** I lend you a dictionary?
Student 2: Yes, please. I haven't got one.

Teacher: **May/Could** I ask you a few questions? I need to know how much you understand.

Student 1: **Shall** I help you with those bags? They look very heavy.
Student 2: Oh, yes, please.

8 May I borrow your pen? – Shall I go to the check-in desk first? – Could you tell me which terminal I need? – What shall I do with this empty bottle?

9 The lessons: **The best way to learn**
Afternoon activities: **What else can you do?**
How old are the students: **Who are the courses for?**

10 1. They talk, listen and have fun.
2. Two weeks long.
3. Do sport (play football, volleyball or table tennis) and visit interesting places.
4. No, they needn't. They can also stay in rooms.

11 *Richtige Reihenfolge:* **D – C – A – B**

12 1. This is the last call for flight ZA 1623 to Madrid. All passengers for flight ZA 1623 to Madrid please go to gate 23 now.
→ **Madrid. – Gate 23.**
2. Can Mrs Emma Walton please go to the information desk now. Emma Walton to the information desk, please. Your sister is waiting for you there.
→ **The information desk. – Her sister.**

3. Welcome on our flight to London Heathrow. The flight will take about one hour and 15 minutes today so we hope to land at half past two local time. The weather in London is sunny and warm today – as usual.
→ **One hour fifteen minutes. – Half past two. – Sunny and warm.**

13 Cou<u>l</u>d you please ta<u>l</u>k to him for me? – Hey, you mus<u>t</u>n't stand on his sand cas<u>t</u>le. – People are of<u>t</u>en no<u>t</u> very ca<u>l</u>m at Chris<u>t</u>mas. – Lis<u>t</u>en for ha<u>l</u>f an hour to this beautiful CD.

14 1. **Jill**; 2. **Bill**; 3. **Nina**; 4. **Nina**; 5. **Nina**

Jill: Bill, would you like a cup of tea?
Bill: Yes, I'd love one, please. And could you help me with the dinner, please? The chicken is burning and I haven't done the chips or the salad yet.
Nina: Oh, I can help if you like.
Jill: No, don't worry about it. I'll help him. It can be dangerous in the kitchen when Bill is cooking.
Bill: I heard that.
Nina: Well, shall I lay the table?
Bill: Yes, please, Nina.
Nina: Oh, and what shall I do with this old newspaper?
Jill: Is it a German one?
Nina: Yes.
Jill: Well, can you put it with the other old newspapers in that cupboard, please. Or do you want to read it, Bill?
Bill: Ha ha. Jill's just laughing at me because I did a German course once. And I can read menus and things – but a German newspaper? No, they're too difficult for me.
Nina: Er, may I have a cup of tea, please?
Jill: Oh, yes, of course. Would you like milk and sugar?
Nina: Milk? Do you put milk in tea?
Jill: Yes, of course. Most people in England like milk in their tea.
Nina: Do they? Oh well, could I try it, too, please?
Jill: Yes. Here you are. Do you like it?
Nina: Mm. Yes, it's, er …

15 1. Because the chicken is burning but he hasn't done the chips or the salad yet.
2. She doesn't really like it because it's got milk in, but she says she likes it because she wants to be polite.

Revision C (Unit 6–7)

1

	By air	*On water*	*On land*
Verbs	fly	row	drive
	land	sail	ride
Nouns	departures	ship	train
	flight	ferry	platform
	helicopter	harbour	road

2 1. kind; 2. gentle; 3. friendly; 4. patient; 5. mean

3 speak – sprechen; tell – erzählen; say – sagen; call – rufen; explain – erklären repeat – wiederholen; invite – einladen; shout – schreien, rufen; cry – weinen, schreien, rufen; talk – reden

4 The doctor said that I needed to do more sport so I thought very **hard.** Which sport was **best** for me? I've always liked football. It's really **exciting** but I can't run very **fast.** And rock climbing is even **more exciting** but it's also **scarier.** I'd like to go surfing but I swim **badly.** I'm even **worse** at in-line skating. I tried it once and broke my arm. I thought orienteering was fun but it rains too much here and I can't read maps very **well.** I thought and thought and then I found the **perfect** sport for me. It's **quick** and fun and you needn't run fast or get wet. It's table football!

5
Fiona: **I've just booked** an abseiling trip and I'm a little scared. **Have you ever been?**
Steve: No, **I haven't,** but **I've been** rock climbing and that's almost the same.
Fiona: And **did you like** it?
Steve: Yes, it **was** great fun. It **wasn't** scary at all.
Fiona: And why **didn't you do** it again?
Steve: I **had** an accident and **broke** my arm.
Fiona: But you **said** it wasn't scary.
Steve: No, it wasn't. I just **fell** over somebody's equipment.
Fiona: And **did you fall** down the mountain?
Steve: No, we **were climbing** on the wall in the sports hall.

C   Lösungen

6 Excuse me. **May** I open a window? It's very warm in here. – Yes, OK.
Shall I help you with your bags? – Oh, that's very nice of you. Thanks.
Excuse me, **could** I sit there, please? – Oh, yes, of course, I'll move my bag.

7 It was nine o'clock and I **was lying** on the beach near my house. It **was getting** dark and there was nobody else there. I was looking at the sky when I **saw** a bright light. I **thought** it was a plane but I couldn't hear anything, which was strange. The light got nearer and nearer and I **was getting** very scared when it suddenly went dark.
A moment later the lights were on again and I could see something on the water. It **looked** like a big building. While I **was trying** to get up, a door **opened** and some things came out. I wanted to run away but I couldn't move. They **were moving** across the water when I heard something. Were they trying to talk to me? Then I **heard** something that sounded like French and then Russian and then they said in perfect English, "Can you tell us the way to the planet Zarfee, please? We're lost."

8 If it **rains** tomorrow, I **will stay** in the house all day. If my mum **has** time, **she'll bake** a cake. I **won't be** very happy if I **don't get** any letters. If my friends **remember** my birthday, they **will visit** me.

9 The weather **will be** nice tomorrow and so we**'re going to hike** by the coast. We**'re going to take** our swimming things. I hope the water **won't be** too cold. My mother **is going to meet** us at the end of the walk. I'm sure everybody **will have** a great day. I **won't enjoy** it quite as much though, because Ryan **isn't going to come** with us.

10 Where do you come from? Have you ever been to England before?
Who taught you English? What are you going to do next weekend?

11 <u>Although</u> Jim, my host dad, wanted to take me to the language school in the morning, I went by bus. It was more difficult than I thought. <u>First</u> the bus was <u>thirty minutes</u> late and then I didn't know where to get off <u>because</u> I couldn't see which stop I was at. I got off at the wrong stop, <u>of course</u>. I didn't know which way to walk <u>so</u> I asked a friendly man. He couldn't speak English very well <u>and so</u> he didn't understand the question. <u>Then</u> I asked a <u>nice</u> woman <u>but</u> I couldn't understand her <u>because</u> she spoke so fast. <u>Next</u> I got my <u>old</u> map out of my bag. I was walking down a <u>busy</u> road <u>and looking</u> at the map when I bumped into a <u>beautiful</u> girl <u>who</u> was also reading a map. We both said sorry <u>and then</u> laughed. <u>Luckily</u> she was <u>also</u> going to the language school <u>and so</u> we walked together. She was from Russia <u>and</u> she spoke English badly, too, <u>so</u> I couldn't understand her <u>and</u> she couldn't understand me <u>but</u> we had <u>great</u> fun <u>anyway</u> and talked <u>happily</u> all the way to the language school.

12 *Doctor:* Hello. What happened to you then?
Jenny: I fell off my bike and hurt my head and my arm.
Doctor: Have you got a headache?
Jenny: No, I haven't, but I feel sick.
Doctor: That's the shock. Can you move your arm?
Jenny: Yes, but it hurts when I move my fingers.
Doctor: Well, I don't think you've broken it. Here are some tablets for the pain. Take two tablets three times a day.

13 Cecilia packs wellies ☐, an anorak ☒, one pullover ☒, a compass ☐.

In the east of England it's often rainy ☐, foggy ☐, and cold ☒.

Cecilia is going to go orientiering ☐.

Mum: So have you finished yet?
Cecilia: I think so. Look, my bags are almost full.
Mum: Yes, but you haven't got your anorak. It's hanging on the door.
Cecilia: Oh yes.
Mum: And what about your wellies? It rains in England a lot, you know.
Cecilia: Wellies? Mum, I'm going to London. You don't wear wellies in London and anyway it doesn't rain in London very much. It's only in the west of England that it rains a lot.
Mum: Well, OK, but have you packed any pullovers? It can be very cold in England even in summer.
Cecilia: I've got one pullover. Maybe I'll pack another.
Mum: Are you going to go orienteering while you're there?
Cecilia: I don't think so. I don't think I'll have time.
Mum: Well, maybe you should take your compass anyway. It can get very foggy in London, you know?
Cecilia: Oh Mum, you and your clichés.
Mum: And maybe you should take some food with you, too. The food isn't so good in England either, you know.
Cecilia: Ha ha.

14 Dear Pete,
We're having a great time here in Scotland and the weather has been great, too. It's been sunny every day. We've hiked in the mountains three times and yesterday we went swimming in a loch. That was fun. Tomorrow we're going to go to a ceilidh.
See you next week.
Bye,
Mick

Lösungen

15 Shall I help you with the dinner? – Yes, please. → In a host family.
How much is a travelcard, please? – 5.50. → On the Tube.
Where are the changing rooms? – Over there. → In a clothes shop.
Can you tell me what the special is? – It's cheese pasta. → In a café.
Hey, what's the problem? – He hit me. → Stopping a fight.
Do you feel sick? – No, I don't. → At the doctor's.
Have you got any special ones? – No, we haven't. → At the post office.

Boy: Shall I help you with the dinner?
Woman: Yes, please. Do you know what time your course starts tomorrow?
Boy: Yes, it starts at 9 o'clock and we've got three hours of lessons in the morning.

Woman: How much is a travelcard, please?
Man: 5.50 for three zones.
Woman: OK. I'd like a travelcard, please, and can you tell me how I get to Buckingham Palace?

Girl: Can I try on these trousers and T-shirts, please?
Woman: Yes, but you can only take three things into the changing rooms.
Girl: OK. And where are the changing rooms, please?
Woman: Over there.

Boy: Can you tell me what the special is?
Woman: It's cheese pasta.
Boy: OK, I'd like the pasta and my friend would like the chicken and chips, please.

Woman: Hey, what's the problem?
Girl: He hit me.
Woman: Well, stop it, both of you, and you can talk about it.

Doctor: Do you feel sick?
Boy: No, I don't, but I've got a terrible headache.

Girl: How much are stamps to America?
Woman: They're 92 pence.
Girl: Have you got any special ones?
Woman: No, we haven't.